FLYING SECTION 17

FLYING SECTION 17

By
HAUPT HEYDEMARCK

Translated by
CLAUD W. SYKES

The Naval & Military Press Ltd

Published by

The Naval & Military Press Ltd
Unit 5 Riverside, Brambleside
Bellbrook Industrial Estate
Uckfield, East Sussex
TN22 1QQ England

Tel: +44 (0)1825 749494

www.naval-military-press.com
www.nmarchive.com

In reprinting in facsimile from the original, any imperfections are inevitably reproduced and the quality may fall short of modern type and cartographic standards.

DEDICATED TO MY FORMER SECTION COMMANDER,
CAPTAIN MAX MOHR

HAUPT HEYDEMARCK,
Captain (retired).

CONTENTS

CHAPTER		PAGE
I.	Taking the Air	11
II.	Blind Man's Buff	16
III.	A Virgin Flight	22
IV.	Archie!	27
V.	A Labour of Love	32
VI.	Heinrich	37
VII.	The Gale	41
VIII.	Good Shot!	50
IX.	Spätzle	54
X.	A Painful Predicament	60
XI.	The Squadron Flight	66
XII.	Shot Down	74
XIII.	Honouring a Hero	67
XIV.	P.G.	92
XV.	The Red Machine	104
XVI.	My Little Bluff	109
XVII.	Escape!	118
XVIII.	Merely by the Way	127
XIX.	A Good Slice of Bad Luck	131
XX.	The Ace of Châlons	135
XXI.	School for Greenhorns	140
XXII.	The Luck of the Clouds	145
XXIII.	Must be Done	151
XXIV.	Done!	157
XXV.	Through Thick and Thin	162

LIST OF ILLUSTRATIONS

FACING PAGE

THE AUTHOR . . . FRONTISPIECE
1. A FRIEND IN THE AIR 16
2. THE LANDING MARK AT ATTIGNY AERODROME 17
3. TAKE ENGMANN 20
4. CUMULI ON A STRATUS CEILING . . . 21
5. A CLOUD PLAIN 28
6. BERGER'S MACHINE CAMOUFLAGED AGAINST OBSERVATION BY ENEMY AIRCRAFT . . 29
7. STRUT HIT BY SHRAPNEL FUSE . . . 32
8. LIEUTENANT RATY'S CAPTURED NIEUPORT . 33
9. TAKE ENGMANN FLYING OVER THE LINES AT 4,000 METRES 48
10. CAUDRON TWO-SEATER 49
11. SPÄTZLE'S MACHINE AFTER A FIGHT . . 64
12. SPÄTZLE IN HOSPITAL 65
13. LARGE MACHINE BELONGING TO THE GERMAN FIGHTER SQUADRON 68
14. REMAINS OF THE MACHINE BERGER DESTROYED AFTER LANDING 69
15. BERGER AND STATTAUS, WITH THE FRENCH COMMANDANT 76
16. STATTAUS AND BERGER ON THE WAY TO THEIR EXAMINATION 77
17. BERGER'S LAST CRASH 96
18. GOY'S MACHINE AFTER BEING PATCHED UP . 97
19. A CLOUD CEILING CLOSING UP . . . 112
20. THE "AIRMAN'S SUN" REFLECTED UPON AN UPPER CLOUD CEILING , , , . 113

LIST OF ILLUSTRATIONS

	FACING PAGE
21. ATTIGNY AERODROME, WITH THE NEW HANGARS	132
22. SIDE VIEW FROM THE OBSERVER'S SEAT.	133
23. CORPORAL FINKS AND LIEUTENANT FREYTAG	140
24. THE MACHINE THAT LOST ITS UNDERCARRIAGE	141
25. LANCE-CORPORAL SCHATTAT (ON THE RIGHT)	144
26. CUMULI.	145
27. A RAIN GUST; FRESCO ON MESSROOM WALL	148
28. THE NEW RAILWAY LINE	149
29. RAIN CLOUDS	156
30. NIEUPORT, WITH PIVOTABLE MACHINE-GUN	157
31. WING OF THE AUTHOR'S MACHINE, PITTED WITH BULLET SPLINTERS	160
32. NEW RAILWAY JUNCTION AT COOLUS	161

CHAPTER I

TAKING THE AIR

I HAD been transferred to Flying Section 17 at Attigny. "When can I fly my first long distance reconnaissance?" I asked. Captain Mohr laughed. "Not at present. First you'll slip along this side of the front and have a look at our 3rd Army's sector from above. As Barth is going on leave, you can fly with his pilot, Stattaus."

"And then I shall be permanently allotted to a machine?"

The captain nodded. "Yes—if you're not shot down first."

When the weather clears up in the afternoon, we climb into our box of tricks and taxi to the edge of the aerodrome.

Slowly Stattaus pushes his throttle open—the buzz of the engine rises to a low howl—our bird hops laboriously across the meadow—lifts her tail—wobbles on both wheels over some rough patches of ground—her speed grows faster and faster—a bit of a jump—whoops! she lifts herself off the ground—we are flying!

I turn round. I look at the long row of tents and sheds down below, with their flags fluttering gaily in the breeze. As we go into a turn, the little town looms up. Soldiers and peasants stare up at us inquisitively.

From Rethel we follow the straight line of the Rheims road. A lorry column is on its way to the front; the little square vehicles stand out against the silver-grey ribbon of the road. Each lorry raises a cloud of dust, which the breeze wafts languidly over the fields.

There is also some traffic on the line. A long goods train steams out of Neuflize station, but we soon leave it behind us. Meanwhile we have climbed to 2,000 metres.

The road crosses a wood and dives into the fruitful valley of the Suippe. The fields are covered with a medley of white debris—dummy trenches, where our troops are being drilled into storming operations.

A look ahead—the lines. A grey strip between

friend and foe—No-Man's-Land. Here the front trenches are a thousand metres away from each other —there they are converging. Saps push out towards one another like groping tentacles.

No more trails of smoke on the railway. No more vehicles or pedestrians on the road. This is the domain of the artillery.

The village over yonder has hardly one outer wall left intact. There are just a few inside walls of the houses still standing. The soil is pockmarked with thousands and thousands of shell-holes; near the front trenches it has been so torn by shells and mines that broad strips of the naked chalk are left exposed.

Rheims. The cathedral rises up as a mighty landmark from the narrow streets.

Climbing to 2,500, we bear off eastwards, and I note the landscape and the lie of the lines. My first front patrol! Full of joyful expectations, I hover around the threshold that I may not cross to-day—yonder, bathed in the gleaming sun, lies the promised land where I shall make my first flight over enemy territory to-morrow. My eyes peer out far to southward, where railways and canals, roads and paths, camps and columns, stations and quays await me—and Archies and enemy airmen as well.

Suddenly Stattaus turns to me and points to the right with a waving hand; over Auberive white cloudlets of bursting Archie shells are forming out of the air. They come from German guns, and can therefore only be intended for a French machine.

At him!

But our ambition remains unrealized. There is no

sign of any *aviateur*, when we reach the windstrewn shellbursts a few minutes later. We fly on despondently. But I quickly regain my spirits. A machine hangs in the air over Somme-Py, barely 1,000 metres away from us. German or French? As we are flying towards one another, I cannot make him out with my glasses.

Feverish excitement!

At last he curves away—and the black cross greets me... sharply defined against its white background. A comrade! We wave to one another gaily. (Photograph 1.)

Onward! All quiet in the air. Nothing in particular going on below, it seems; only a sudden flash from the cannon mouth every now and then, followed by the burst of a shell. Their detonations are swallowed up in the roar of our engine.

My first job is finished as soon as we reach the dark woods of the Argonne.

" Home again! "

Stattaus bears off northward and takes the throttle-lever back a few pegs. We descend earthwards in a prolonged glide, so as to give our ears a chance to get accustomed to the increasing air pressure. After a fight in the air that involves numerous dives one can hardly catch a single word when one lands. On one occasion Freytag got an inflammation of the middle ear, while I went home with a torn and thickened eardrum.

We follow the valley of the Aisne until our aerodrome looms up between the bracing wires. Two dwarfs flit across the green meadow, unrolling a long linen cloth on the grass ; a broad strip crosses it—the landing mark. (Photograph 2.)

Stattaus throttles right down. Lower and lower we glide—now we are hovering just above the grass—slowly our bird sinks—bump—the wheels touch—the tail a second later—we taxi fifty metres—and come to a standstill.

A good landing !

CHAPTER II

BLIND MAN'S BUFF

I FLEW with Stattaus for four months. Then I had to give him up to Heinrich Barth when he returned. I received in his place Sergeant Engmann, nicknamed "Take." He was a skilled locksmith and a true Berliner. In the course of the next few months he became my dearest friend and best comrade. (Photograph 3.)

. . . . .

In spite of the enemy's numerical superiority our

1. A Friend in the Air.

2. The Landing Mark at Attigny Aerodrome.

BLIND MAN'S BUFF

long-distance reconnaissances were carried out by single machines, which could worm their way through the barrage of anti-aircraft batteries and enemy airmen far more easily than couples or trios. Although we fought at a disadvantage over on the other side—a shot in the engine might force a landing on enemy territory—the French machines only attacked us as a rule when there were several of them about. Thus, for instance, Captain Wolff and his pilot, Acting-Officer Scheidt, were assailed by a Nieuport and three Caudrons over Châlons. After Wolff had fired 360 shots and forced the Nieuport to land, the others made off.

Lieutenant Pieper, who was put to fly with Lance-Corporal Schattat, was less lucky. When fighting two Spads, he got a tracer bullet in his left thigh, which shattered the bone. Schattat brought his observer back safely, but the wound healed so badly that " Pieps " was unable to return to us.

. . . . .

A few days later Engmann and I were down for a second patrol. We took off hurriedly when a black wall of clouds came up in the early afternoon and climbed over the clouds at 1200 metres. They were cumuli, and floated on a stratus like icebergs.

(Photograph 4.)

We steered southward by the compass.

Unfortunately, in the haste of our departure I was unable to get a wind report and so had to trust to my instinct. When Take announced: " crossed the lines," I whacked him on to a south-east course. Suddenly he began to wave his hand and pointed to something ahead of us.

"Enemy aircraft!"

Yes there was one crawling about a long way below us. He stood out plainly as a black smudge against the snow-white layer of clouds. I did not need to worry about him; in the first place he was a good 3000 metres below us; in the second he had probably failed to sight us; in the third he was, perhaps, only a two-seater. I decided to find out!

But I soon lowered my glasses; it was only a rift in the clouds. I informed Engmann, and we had a good laugh about it. We were a couple of fine aces, I thought!

Some time later we reached the gaps which allowed me a view of the land below. I saw fields and woods, roads and villages, yes, even a railway—but none of them were old acquaintances. A vague idea dawned on me that my "instinct" had led me farther into enemy country than I meant to go.

The clouds became sparser, and after a while they disappeared. With a quick look round I regained my bearings; the strong nor'-wester had driven us a full twenty kilometres beyond Epernay. The railway junction down there was Fère-Champenoise.

To Châlons!

As the gale was catching us in the flank, we had to allow at least an hour for our flight back to the front.

I had a bit of luck with my fifty-kilo bomb, which I was able to plant on the turn-table of the engine shed. The anti-aircraft gunners were not alarmed until they heard its detonation, and so sent us up a very meagre blessing.

Soon afterwards we reached the first outrunners of

BLIND MAN'S BUFF

the moving cloud-bank. I reduced speed while we could still see the ground below us and made out my compass course for Attigny. Then I whacked Engmann on to it and pointed him out as a further directional guide the shadow of a strut cast by the sun on a lower wing.

"Keep that shadow in its present position," I told him.

When the holes in the clouds became fewer, I had to come to a decision: were we going to keep the machine above the clouds all the way home, or should we drop down through a hole here and fly back below them?

The second solution seemed the least of two evils. Memories of an unhappy adventure in the clouds had left an unpleasantly strong impression on my mind.

A glide with the engine throttled down, I decided.

We had climbed well after dropping our hundredweight bomb and were flying at 3,300. But already the hand of the altimeter was beginning to wander across to the left. I calculated that we must reach the upper ceiling of the clouds at 2,500.

2,300—but the clouds were still a long way below us.

At last we were down to 1,500—but we did not seem to be any nearer those clouds. A bad business! If they reached to within a few hundred metres of the ground, the French would be able to pot at us with their field artillery and machine guns as well as the Archies. So we should have to fly home over the clouds after all.

[1] See *Double-Decker C. 666*, page 33 *et seq.*

While Engmann followed my instructions by opening up a few pegs, I made my calculations. From Suippes to Attigny forty kilometres, and the time was 4.15 p.m. As the wind was slowing us down to eighty-five kilometres an hour, we ought to break through the clouds at 4.43 p.m. and come out over Attigny.

I glanced overboard. The clouds were all banked up together, allowing me no view of the land. They formed a level ceiling, that looked like a field covered with snow. (Photograph 5.)

We plodded on quietly, with the sun shining above us and the snow-white plain below.

Our chronometer showed 4.35 p.m. When I looked out ahead, the surprise I got made me remove my glasses quickly, for someone seemed to have laid a dark ribbon right across the cloud ceiling. The glad certainty dawned on me that there was a wide split in the clouds over the Aisne. And on the Aisne lay Attigny!

I joyfully informed Engmann of my observations. Now we had no need to push through the clouds, but could go down in light and sunshine.

Several minutes later we reached the gap; the river winding its usual course sent a greeting up to welcome us. The little town half-way on our right was Attigny, and to southward of the houses lay the aerodrome. Our aerodrome!

We glided down gaily.

Engmann was so filled with the bliss of homecoming that he forgot to take account of the wind's direction and barged into the aerodrome in a side-wind. Luckily

3. Take Engmann.

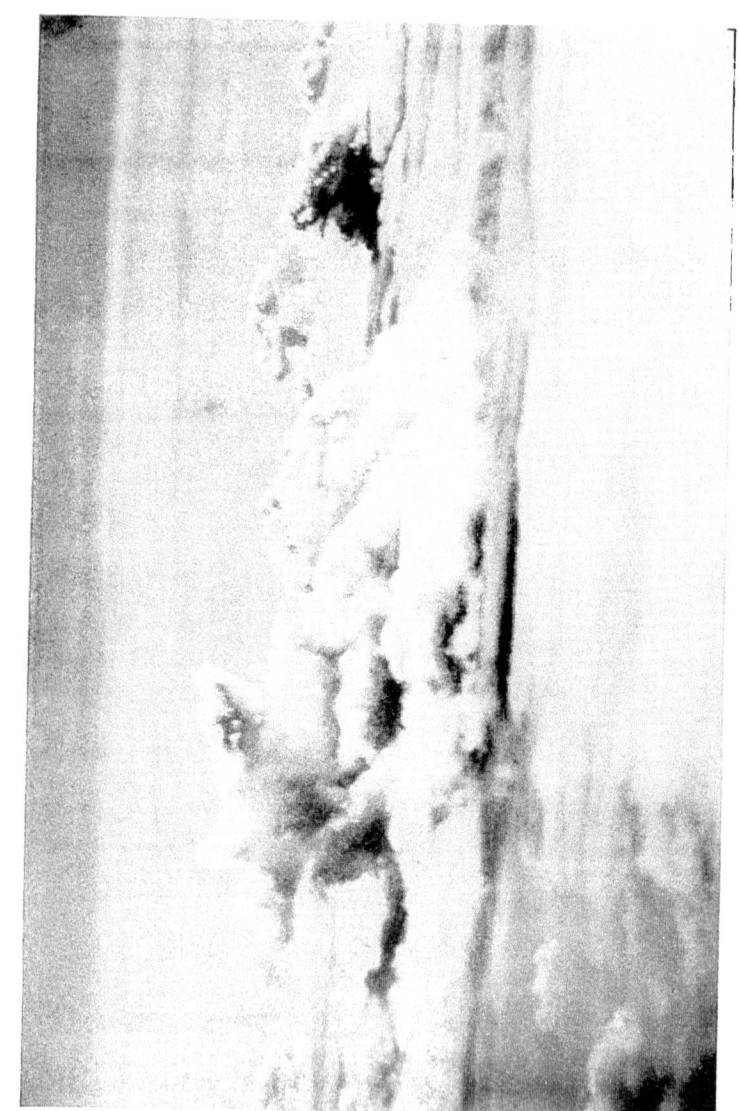

4. Cumuli on a Stratus Ceiling.

I noticed his mistake at the last moment and kept the machine hovering for a good time. At first we touched the ground with one wheel only—then the other came down—our bird put her nose into the wind—taxied off to the left in an ever-narrowing arc—and came to a stop after a short run.

"Take!"

But Engmann was forearmed. "Just what I said the other day," he protested. "They braced her a bit too tight at the last overhaul. That's given her rather a twist to the left—and in addition to that——"

"——in addition to that you landed into a side-wind, my dear boy."

"Yes. I did that as well."

I shook his arm. "You know the old airman's saying :

"If your machine one day starts veering
Against the course that you are steering,
Don't make a grouse of it or say
Your bird has got a twist that way.
Admit what's certain to be true;
The twist, dear pilot, lies in you."

Engmann nodded cheerfully.

CHAPTER III

A VIRGIN FLIGHT

DAY after day I had to issue the bombs to the crews that took off. As the first patrol generally shot off before sunrise—an event which takes place very early in the summer—I did not find those morning hours too golden.

I therefore sympathized genuinely with Lieutenant Berger, the latest observer to join us, because he had to take over this uncomfortable job. On the evening before he did so, he was telling us his experiences at the flying school.

A VIRGIN FLIGHT

"Thank Heaven, I'm back at the front again. It can't be worse here than in the replacement department."

"Had bad luck?"

Berger laughed. "Bad luck? Stacks of it. My very first flight ended with the pilot flattening out too late and cracking our undercarriage off. Result: a clean fracture. Another time he stalled when taking off, so that we shot down and turned over. Same result. Then when I went to the Observers' School at Königsberg, my raw pilots there brought off a double event. No. 1 couldn't get the machine out of a turn, so that we spun down from 1,500 metres and landed in a battered condition. No. 2 got his wheels stuck in some telegraph wires when trying to make a forced landing outside the aerodrome."

Berger's laugh echoed. "So that was two more write-offs!"

I scanned him through screwed-up eyes, as if to say: "You're a lucky fellow, my lad." Then I drank his health.

"Hals und Beinbruch[1] to your virgin flight. And don't shoot one down the first trip. Leave some prizes for us."

He promised to do so.

. . . . . .

I was not due to fly the following day. When I

---

[1] There is no adequate English rendering for this expression, the literal meaning of which is "neck and leg breakage." Like all other flying men, the German aviators at the front had their own superstitions, one of which was that it was fatal to wish a flier "good luck" before he took off. If, however, someone expressed the wish that he might break his neck and legs, he felt tolerably certain of coming back safe and sound. TRANSLATOR'S NOTE.

strolled out to the aerodrome about noon, Captain Mohr rang me up.

"Berger has just been shot down—luckily this side of the lines. Take over his job at once."

Engmann arrived in haste while I was having our machine got out. He made a wry face.

"If they nailed Herr Lieutenant Berger at Rheims, we are sure to get it in the neck at Auberive."

I laughed him out of his gloomy forebodings.

"Why should we? You must do in the air as they do on the ground. Jump straight into the hole the last shell has made, for no others will burst there. The more it stinks, the better for you. And so we'll cross the front at Rheims, just at the spot where they nabbed Lieutenant Berger."

My theory worked out even better in practice than I could have expected. Not only did we slip across without a fight, but there was not a tail to be seen anywhere in the air.

. . . . .

I visited Berger in hospital that afternoon. He was in good spirits and welcomed me with a cheerful grin. As I saw he was in no need of consolation, I joined heartily in his laughter.

"Wasn't it bad luck?"

"You know the old saying: 'A good beginning to the week, as the murderer remarked when they fixed his execution for a Monday.' Well, how did it happen?"

Berger nodded. "A Voisin ran into us over the trenches. He bolted as quick as he could, but his escort went for us. My good Tanneberg nodded when I showed him the Nieuport. The only trouble was that he did not see it; he thought I was pointing out how close the shells were bursting to us. Bad luck!

"When the Frenchman started rattling away at us, my pilot got out of his burst with a turn as soon as he had recovered from the first moments of his surprise. But our main tank was badly holed, so that the engine began to sputter. It stopped when we gave it the petrol from the gravity tank.

"But meanwhile the Nieuport was attending to us again and put some hits into me. When I fired, he put his machine into a nosedive; then he zoomed up and shot our engine in pieces from below."

"And you could not get at him in the dead angle?"

Berger laughed. "No. When I tried to shoot straight down at him, my machine-gun promptly jammed. And my Mauser automatic had got hit twice in the barrel."

"But couldn't your pilot pot him with his machine-gun?"

Berger made a sorrowful face. "We were flying the old machine that doesn't carry a forward gun. So we put the machine on to her nose and shot down across the lines. Our dive was so steep that I thought Tanneberg was hit and we were out of control. In any case we managed to slip the Frenchman at last, and came down somewhere near Epoy with our prop standing still. We took a young telegraph post with us when we made our forced landing, and there's one of its china insulators still sticking in the engine casing. Then we camouflaged the machine against aircraft and balloons with branches; otherwise those Frenchies would have shot it in pieces with their long-barrelled guns." (Photograph 6.)

I congratulated him on his good luck.

"But you're not exactly a comradely fellow. You've hardly taken over the job of O.C. bombs before you get yourself shot down so as to slide out of it. All the same I'm sorry you got knocked about so badly."

Berger protested energetically. "That's nothing! Only a few scratches and a hole in my foot, which is already beginning to heal up."

"Just a flesh wound, then?"

He shook his head. "I shouldn't have let them bring me here for that. No, one bullet went through the middle bone of the foot. The other ten only grazed me." He pointed out the wounds: "Here—fingers, shoulders, legs, but all of them just scratches."

Great was now my amazement. "Ten hits? Man alive, you can go to the circus and stand in front of the board for a drunken knife-thrower after that. Nothing will happen to you!"

Berger laughed. "My childhood's guardian angel, I always say! I'll be back again in a couple of weeks, and then I'll take the bombs off you."

. . . . .

But thus it came to pass.

Berger had to wait a good three months before he returned to the section. I regret to say that Tanneberg fell in action shortly afterwards.

CHAPTER IV

ARCHIE!

EVERYONE has some sort of a bee in his bonnet. I was said to have been " bitten by a mad bomb," because I always took " eggs " with me, even without orders, while Casparito had Archies on the brain. Casparito's real name was Caspar Boormann, reserve captain in the First Guards Field Artillery, temporarily attached to No. 17 as an observer. Heinrich Barth refined his name to Casparito, because he was of slender build.

His speciality was the anti-aircraft batteries and most

especially those at Ste Ménehould. Whenever he returned from a flight over the lines, the topic of conversation was always the same. One example will serve:

"Well, Casparito, what was it like?"

"Thick air! They've planted a couple of new Archies at Ste Ménehould again—north of the railway station."

"Were there any clouds?"

But Casparito was too engrossed in his pet subject to take in my question. "Two new Archies. They appear to be mounted in a sandpit."

"Lively rail traffic?"

"And the brutes shot magnificently. They actually made a record hit."

He led me to his machine. "Look there—a shrapnel fuse bang on the strut." (Photograph 7.)

I rejoiced with him at this honourable scar. "Marvellous! Any fights?"

"And the dirtiest trick is that the old Archie battery in the town is still carrying on. I did hope they'd at least remove that one. Not they! They bracketed me when I flew over the station."

"Seen any aircraft?"

"On the other hand the Châlons Archies didn't fire a shot to-day. I thought about them for a long time. Why this bashfulness? Probably they couldn't get my range well, because I was flying in the sun."

"Most interesting! And the railway traffic?"

Love's labour lost!

"But the very meanest trick of all is that our

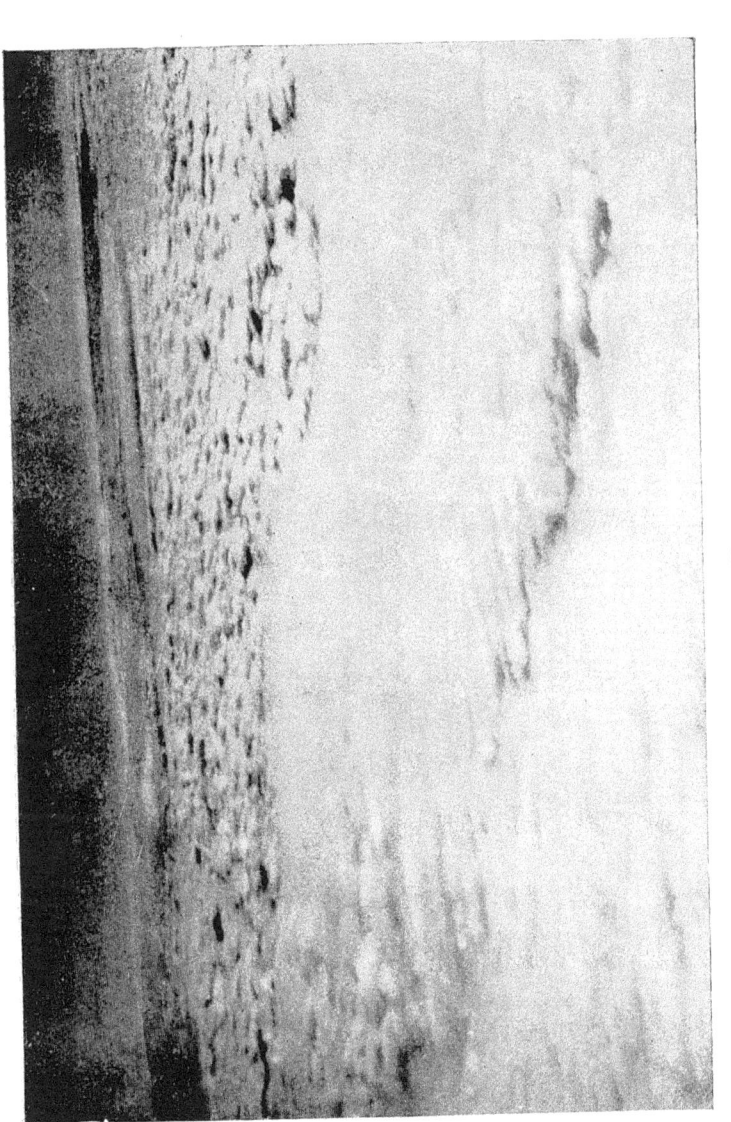

5. A Cloud Plain.

6. Berger's Machine Camouflaged against Observation by Enemy Aircraft.

ARCHIE!

Archieless stretch round Rheims is now filled up. For at Verzenay——"

Then I gave it up.

. . . . .

Moreover Boormann's affection for the French Archies was by no means one-sided; it was returned most cordially, though hardly platonically. When a single shrapnel from the new battery at Verzenay put at least fourteen hits on to his machine, he thought he had climbed the pinnacle of bliss. But things always went one better in our flights over the lines, as Boormann was also destined to find out. He got a shrapnel bullet in the knee joint—this time from one of his favourite children at Ste Ménehould. His friends there did not mean to be rude; it was to be taken as just an amicable if somewhat boisterous joke on their part that the bullet missed the bone and penetrated deep into the flesh.

. . . . .

My face grew thoughtful as I strolled out to the aerodrome one morning. A thick ground-mist had risen. I was called to the telephone.

"Mohr speaking. Morning! Boormann took off at 4.15, and not back yet. Please let off a few fogbombs."

The starting crews planted the barrel in the ground a couple of minutes later. In went one of the big "radishes." The match was lit—everyone stepped back several paces—and the heavy thing whizzed into the air with a peal of thunder. The detonations of the bursting bomb did not reach us till several seconds later.

I also put out two red lights and a green one for a landing triangle. As a matter of fact I had very little hope of their penetrating the thick layer of fog, but better to do a bit too much than a bit too little.

We listened eagerly for the drone of an engine. In vain! Several minutes later we sent up another "radish."

Meanwhile it was eight o'clock. As Casparito had only to fly the middle stretch of our sector, he ought to have been back long before that. So he was overdue! There was, however, some hope that he might have made an intermediary landing. I rang up all the aerodromes.

Result: reported missing.

At last, at last—well past nine—the telephone operator brought the news. "Aircraft made a forced landing at Saulces Champenoises."

No further particulars were forthcoming. So off we went as quickly as possible. I took the two aerodrome attendants and the ambulance N.C.O. in a car to his landing place.

Unfortunately my fears were justified. Our men had had hard fights with three Nieuports and a Caudron over Châlons. Corporal Kretzschmar got a bullet in his right leg, after it had gone right through the tank. Luckily it did not touch the bone. Boormann was intact. The machine looked very nice, with twelve hits on it.

. . . . .

When Boormann was to be transferred to another section, we heard rumours that he had proposed to some girl during the preliminary leave he enjoyed. As

No. 17 was composed of hardened bachelors—with the exception of Pieps, who had got himself engaged in the meanwhile—something had to be done about it. The chief addressed the two candidates for marriage with a grave face.

"I hope you did not think it over seriously first."

Casparito laughed. "Oh, yes, we did. Very seriously."

Mohr shook his head in disapproval.

"But that is quite wrong. Many people say you ought to think it over if you want to get married. But if you think it over, you don't get married. So the only thing is not to think it over."

We were bound to admit he was right.

CHAPTER V

A LABOUR OF LOVE

VISITING our Fokker Staffel one afternoon, I was able to join in welcoming an involuntary guest, Lieutenant Jean Raty. He was caught in quite a curious way.

His squadron was attacked by our scouts. Their leader, Lieutenant Student, buttonholed Monsieur Raty's one-seater. When he saw him sideslip and turn over several times as he went down, he left him to Lieutenant Esser, who had just arrived on the scene. But Raty was not hit; he merely got a bit nervous when changing an ammunition drum, and so sideslipped. As his engine went dead in the course of his involuntary aerobatics, there was nothing left for him but to land.

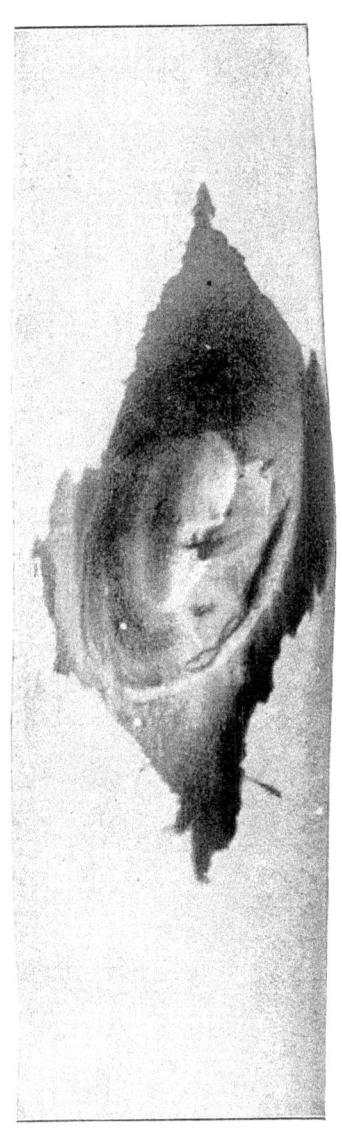

7. Strut hit by Shrapnel Fuse.

8. LIEUTENANT RATY'S CAPTURED NIEUPORT.

A LABOUR OF LOVE

Esser put his machine down close by and relieved the French pilot of his matches before shaking hands. With a smile of resignation the little lieutenant pointed to a number of matches lying on the ground. All were duds, and so he was unable to fire his machine. (Photograph 8.)

After coffee had been served the Frenchman wrote the following letter to his comrades:

> To the captain commanding the Nieuport Squadron, No. 38, at Châlons:
>
> After taking part in his first fight over Mezières, Sub-lieutenant Raty attacked three Fokkers in order to help a Caudron. Having exhausted his ammunition and having been forced down to 200 metres he was forced to land on account of his machine-gun jamming.
>
> He is safe and sound. He has received much kindness from the pilots of the Fokker Staffel.
>
> He requests you to inform M. Perchot, rue de l'Abbé de l'Epée 16, Paris, and Mlle Darnys, rue de Tocqueville 67, Paris.
>
> With greetings to all his comrades,
>
> JEAN RATY.
>
> June 16, 1916.

I gladly took charge of the letter and promised to despatch it to the right address.

. . . . .

Soon afterwards Engmann and I had to fly to Châlons on reconnaissance work. It was a welcome opportunity to discharge my comradely duty by dropping Raty's letter down. I stowed it in a bag which was provided with long streamers that would be easily seen when it fell. Then followed a brief discussion with Take Engmann.

"We shall cross the lines east of Rheims and fly straight to Châlons. With this strong north-west wind blowing I shall have to keep a couple of kilometres in reserve to make sure that the letter drops in the town and gets found. We'll bomb the station at the same time."

. . . . .

The Archies at the front appear to guess our courier's job and content themselves with a bare dozen shells.

We reach Châlons via the Ferme de Metz. While still a good way from the boundaries of the town I drop my bag, which has been weighted with sand. As it falls, the red, white, and black streamers shoot upward stiffly.

A heavy barrage makes the flight to the station very uncomfortable. When at last my bombs land neatly between the railway lines, the streamers attached to the bag are still waving in the breeze.

I glance back while Take bears off north-eastward. At this moment all the population—except the over-timid, who still crouch in their cellars—will be staring up at us and thus be certain to catch sight of the bag floating down from above. The purpose of my manœuvre is accomplished.

The hits made by our bombs seem to have spurred the ambition of the Archies, but the wind is pushing us eastward so strongly that the shellbursts lie too wide on our left. We are out of range before the gunners have worked out the corrections.

A LABOUR OF LOVE

The second part of our task is to photograph the stations of the Noblette-Auve railway. After making the first exposures I search the air for enemy aircraft.

Lo and behold—a Nieuport!

He has sneaked up to within 800 metres of us. I swing my machine-gun round expectantly.

He could easily overhaul us in his swift one-seater —but he does not appear anxious to do so. Probably he has the usual dislike of single-handed attacks and is waiting to see if any of his comrades will come along.

We make for Somme-Bionne when I have Auve on my plates. The Archies cease fire, so as to avoid endangering their compatriot.

My job is finished when I have got a serial picture of the camp. I am free to devote myself again to the bashful wooer, who has been following us for more than a quarter of an hour. If he had been an Englishman, I should have imagined he had made a bet with some comrade that he could force us back over the lines without firing a shot—simply by power of suggestion. But such haughty aloofness does not fit that theory. Has he forgotten his ammunition? Or has he an incurable jam?

I am bursting with curiosity. He really must be made to show his real intentions. Brief instructions to Engmann: turn round to attack!

But before we have completed our turn, the valiant little fellow puts his machine down and makes off southward in a nosedive. We laugh heartily.

"Better be a coward for five minutes than dead for life!"

The Frenchman has hardly buzzed off before a murderous Archie fire starts. The batteries that hitherto dared not shoot on account of the Nieuport spew up all the contents of their barrels.

Down goes our machine on to her nose until the anemometer records 200 kilometres. What does it matter how far down our drive takes us—we are going home!

CHAPTER VI

HEINRICH

AFTER our evening meal we generally remained chatting in the mess. As we had a number of interests in common, it was only natural that certain topics of conversation cropped up again and again. As Germans are an order-loving nation, we divided them into twelve subjects and gave them numbers.

The most popular were:

    Subject 1 : Service.
    Subject 3 : Weather.
    Subject 6 : Food.

Subject 7 : Girls.
Subject 9 : Orders and Decorations.
Subject 12 : Cursing one's superiors.

The last-mentioned had a subdivision 12a : Cursing the bombs one had to take up.

* * * * *

The service-book went the round.

"First patrol : Captain Linke and Lieutenant Steinbrenner." Then came the details of the job, which ended : " 50-kilo bomb on Châlons station."

As the rain rattling against the window in a lovely rhythm promised "airman's weather" for the morrow, our skipper donned the red cap which an Austrian cavalryman gave him when he was on the Eastern Front. This was the signal for immunity for speakers, which even liberated the ticklish sub-subject 12a.

Steinbrenner, the Swabian whom we had christened "Spätzle" on account of his nationality, opened the discussion.

"This damned bombing business! It takes us hours to screw ourselves up to the right height!"

Two parties of pros and cons were quickly formed. Casparito and I were the only two besides Captain Mohr who represented the "pro" with any conviction.

"In any case it's fun to worry the French!"

"You've got to hit them first!"

"Even when you fly past without dropping anything or if you've not got a bomb with you, they look up in a blue funk and wonder what you'll do."

Freytag was an uncompromising opponent.

"And what follows? The French army H.Q. at

Châlons, that wants its peace and quiet, is always putting up new Archie batteries and setting its Jagdstaffels at us more fiercely."

Barth agreed with him. "Our job is long-distance reconnaissance. The way you people use your bombs is the very thing to spoil them. The more hits you make, the more obstacles you create."

"You're right, Heinrich. If we didn't bomb, the big noises in Châlons wouldn't be so interested in us."

Barth pursed his lips into a smile. "Yes, my lads —but all the same it gives you quite a pleasant feeling when one of those eggs drops bang into a nest."

Nevertheless, Reserve-lieutenant Heinrich Barth, who in civilian life is a partner in a big commercial firm, was soon driven into the camp of the uncompromising anti-bombers by a very regrettable incident.

. . . . .

Contrary to expectations the rain-clouds cleared away during the night, thus enabling Linke and Steinbrenner to take off.

When I strolled into the photographic department about noon, I found Spätzle examining his snaps.

"That's my bomb," he said. "We aimed at the station, but the side-wind deflected it. All the same it found a good mark." With a grin he handed me the print and the magnifying glass.

"You can see it quite plainly."

White smoke was issuing from a building near the station. Steinbrenner beamed.

"There's smoke enough!" he observed.

"Not smoke, but steam. Probably you hit a boiler."

Spätzle was satisfied. "What a pity we can't find out what sort of a building it was. Being so near the station, it was probably a military concern of some sort."

. . . . .

A few days later a newspaper paragraph gave us the information. Heinrich, who was reading the *Matin*, which I took in *via* Switzerland, after dinner one night, suddenly jumped up and raised his glass.

"Never again will I carry a bomb without express orders. I have no desire to assist in my own ruin. I hereby drink my deepest contempt of you, my dear Spätzle!"

In answer to our chorus of "Hallos" he read the report:

"Châlons-sur-Marne. On Saturday morning a German aeroplane flew over the town and dropped a bomb which destroyed the brewery."

Then he continued:

"The brewery which Spätzle has destroyed in an act of abysmal folly owes our firm 1,500 francs—and now we can whistle for our money."

But Steinbrenner showed himself to be a perfect gentleman.

"My dear Heinrich," he said, "I shall naturally do the right thing. I shall pay you back the whole sum —in monthly instalments of fifty pfennigs."

CHAPTER VII

THE GALE

THE grim easterly gale tries to capsize our machine as she is being brought out of her shed. Only after our united forces have turned her nose into the wind can the mechanics handle her by themselves. Engmann shakes his head in displeasure.

"I don't like it," he says.

"Think I do either? And the ground wind was only three metres a second when they took the measurement this morning! I have sent to the meteorologicals for another measurement. The frogs[1] wanted to push up a balloon at once."

"What's our orders?"

I held my map-board under his nose. "Luckily nothing big. To find out how far they've built the new by-pass railway in the Noblette-Auve valley."

Engmann breathed a sigh of relief. "One consolation, at least, that we needn't go as far as Châlons. I don't feel at all safe to-day, and shall be glad when we're down again."

While he was climbing into his front seat, the armoury master arrived with the new wind report: 10 metres a second on the ground, blowing from east, and 22 metres a second at 2,000, blowing from south.

"Why a report only up to 2,000?" I ask.

The armoury master grins. "When they tried to go higher, the balloon burst. The folk at the station want to know if they're to send up another."

I decide to do without; we cannot wait.

Off!

. . . . .

A windgust lifts us off the ground when we have taxied thirty metres. The sigh of relief I have commenced is broken off when the gust's power is exhausted a few seconds later and lets us drop. But before the wheels can touch the ground, another gust lifts us on to its shoulders and bears us aloft.

Having climbed to 2,500 metres when we reach Vouziers, we can fly straight to the front. Our machine is climbing the gale like a monkey.

[1] Frog = Laubfrosch, slang term for the Field Meteorological Station. Derived from the German habit of keeping a frog in a jar as a weather prophet. TRANSLATOR'S NOTE.

THE GALE

I can let my eyes go wandering while we fight our way forward to the western edge of the Argonne. A car leaves the town in the direction of Monthois. I cannot believe my eyes; it is running faster than we can fly. Such a disgrace for us!

I get a mild shock when I have checked our speed by the ground. We are traversing the countryside at the rate of barely sixteen kilometres an hour, i.e., at the pace of a cyclist out on a Sunday jaunt. As the headwind against us up here is blowing at a speed faster than that of an express train, it is only natural that the road-louse below is making quicker progress than we are!

I take no heed of the earnest warnings given me by friend Küngolt; being an incorrigible optimist, I do not worry about the near future—which will be governed by the shells and shrapnel on the other side of the lines—but rejoice in the distant future—in the homeward flight with the wind behind us, when we can whizz along at a speed of more than 230 kilometres an hour.

4,000! We have never climbed so quickly before.

Certainly we don't get away with anything. What we gain in climbing speed, we lose in forward progress. That doesn't matter, behind our own lines—but the cloven hoof will become manifest on the other side when the Archies pepper us poor snails of the air. What a pity there are no clouds about, in which we could slink past the anti-aircraft batteries at the front! To-day my machine-gun is an unpleasant accessory, because the ammunition drum increases the wind-resistance very considerably. To lessen it, I swing the pivot round and bring the narrow side in the direction of our flight.

Slowly, infinitely slowly we push across the German reserve positions. Nearer and nearer comes the broad strip of land that is mangled by shells and ripped by mines. Then we pass over No-Man's-Land.

The altimeter records 4,600.

The pine woods of the Argonne show up darkly on our left. A light ribbon marks the line where the trenches cross them—the ditch of death between two hunting grounds. And there—snow-white against the background of the pines—come the first two cloudlets from the Archies!

I draw a deep breath. A good thing they have started at last. And bad marksmanship, messieurs! All the same I shall pay you the compliment of running away from your bursts.

We go into a short right-hand turn, and then straight ahead once more.

Now the gunner says: "Ah ha, they don't like that."

He thinks his elevation is good—he'll stick to it—and so we can easily sneak past him.

An unpleasant miaow follows:

"Fee—e—e—e! Fee—e—e—e!"

Two shrapnels! Their smoke streamers waft over to us, betraying the fact that they also come from the Argonne.

As we can crawl along so slowly to-day, it is not long before they feel their way to us.

"Rrrack! Rrrack!"

The shells are also so close that their noise drowns the roar of our engine.

"Fee—e—e—e! Fee—e—e—e!"

The thrust of one of the shrapnels hurtles close by us. At the same time there is a sharp knock on the floor of the cockpit. When I stare suspiciously at the boards by my feet, I see a hole as large as a cherry, and it was not there before. A hit!

Left hand turn. And so the next bursts lie somewhat farther away.

"Rrack!"

Now they are on the mark again.

"Rrrack! Rrrack!"

A hard fist smites our bird so vigorously from below that she is hurled upward, only to flop again the next moment. The engine is untouched; a splinter has merely passed through one of the wings.

Four shells—one of which went quite close!

I cannot blame Engmann for putting the machine into another turn. He is right, and yet he is wrong. It is true that he has to go into the turn so as to avoid making things too easy for the men below—but he ought not to do it, because it forces us backwards.

"Rrrrack!"

They have felt their way up quite close to us. The last shell burst so near to the machine that its air-pressure simply pushed us to one side. If I had not turned the machine-gun round just before, I should have got a shell splinter as large as my hand in my skull.

The military adage is right:

> Good when on the ground it lies,
> But bad when into your mouth it flies.
> Inscription: shell splinter.

When changing drums, I scan the air for enemy machines. But it appears to be free of them.

Then come four other very near detonations. As long as the headwind and our turns are nailing us to this spot, the Archies will not let us slip through their fingers. If things go on like this, we can stop here till our petrol is done—provided we are not brought down first. We must try another way.

Shall we give it up and fly back, to the accompaniment of the Frenchmen's scornful laughter? Out of the question!

Then fly back and cross the lines somewhere else? That would merely mean a similar tragedy.

The only other alternative: to open out and dive down to the devil. We can afford to sacrifice 2,000 of our 4,800 metres.

"Fee—e—e!"

The shrapnel battery has got its teeth into us again. So now for it!

I give Engmann a brisk rub between his shoulders, following it with a whack on his helmet. That means: straight ahead—no turns—dive! I cannot give him any verbal instructions because the wind would push us back the moment he cut his engine.

Engmann puts the machine on to her nose and pulls his throttle-lever slowly back so as not to strain her too much.

Silly of him! We shan't make any progress that way. Open out full! I tap his forehead and make the motion with outstretched hand: "Open your throttle!"

His eyes stare at me dubiously through his goggles:

THE GALE

"Nosedive with engine full on—wings break—crash!"

When I shout my wrath into his ear, he is deeply offended, but obeys and puts the machine down with the engine full on. The thick pointer of the rev. counter shivers to the right.

1,500 . . . 1,600 . . . 1,700

Good! I thrust my outspread hand forward and make a couple of joyous beats: "Leave it at that!"

The gale rages through our bracing wires until they scream.

Altimeter?

4,200!

I lean overboard.

Yes, now we are going forward! At last, at last the ground below us is slipping away at a decent pace.

A glance behind. We are getting through. The shrapnel and shells are not only bursting behind us, but—as we have lost height—above us as well.

When I whoop our war-cry in wild glee, Engmann joins in so mightily that we drown the roar of the engine and the howls of the control wires. When our lungs are empty, we laugh and display our teeth to one another. Shall we not rejoice at having pulled our heads out of the lion's mouth? (Photograph 9.)

The lion's jaws still gape greedily behind us. But the average gunner's usual dislike of drastic range corrections helps us now, for not one single burst comes near us.

We continue to bite our way into the enemy's land. Already the communication trenches are well behind us.

3,400!

Our precious height melts like snow in sunshine. Away with it! The main thing is that we do our job!

And—we do it!

Ste Ménehould comes slowly towards us. Yonder lies the station, and close to it there is an evil battery. To prevent it obtaining any fun out of us, I refrain from flying directly over the lines and content myself with a slanting photograph. I shall get quite a decent picture this way, since there is no haze in the air.

We go into a trifle of a right hand turn in order to get in contact with the new line over Dampierre.

We push our way slowly across country. I rejoice to find no hostile *aviateur* in view. Technically speaking, it is sheer madness to fly in this gale, but from a tactical point of view the flight is remunerative. In the distance I spy a trail of smoke between Bussy-le-Château and St. Remy-sur-Bussy—the first engine on the new line! Also rolling-stock on sidings. Good photos will supplement the observations of my eyes.

All the same I am glad when we see the line run into Cuperly. Our job is done.

I let Engmann cut his engine while a few shells are bursting at a good distance away and sing the song of the wanderer in his ear:

"Homeward! Ho—o—ome—wa—ard!"

Take bears off joyfully to northward and gives his imitation of a polar bear by waggling his head from right to left and back again from left to right. Now our enemy has turned into a friend, for the south wind sits on our backs and drives us across the land-

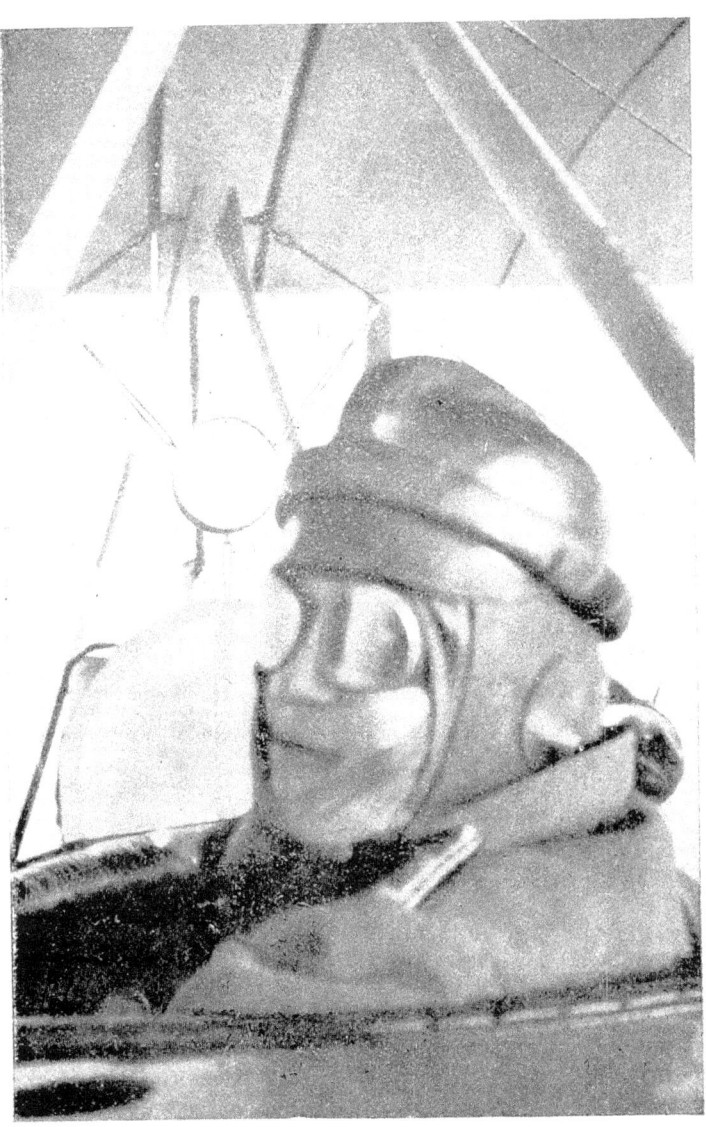
9. TAKE ENGMANN FLYING OVER THE LINES AT 4,000 METRES.

10. CAUDRON TWO-SEATER.

scape at 230 kilometres an hour. We whirl over the front after a bare five minutes, and eight minutes later we reach Attigny.

The gale also demonstrates its benevolence when we land; no deceitful gusts bash us down at the last moment. After a taxi-run that is ideal in its brevity our machine comes to a standstill on the aerodrome once more.

Engmann gives me a joyous side-glance as he rubs his skull and forehead. "The Herr Lieutenant writes quite a Heydemarckish fist," he observes.

I wave his remark aside with a deprecating gesture. " Such little differences are the salt of a happy marriage," I reply. " In the case in question they should not occur again."

Take nods. "And so say I!"

. . . . .

In the afternoon I had to go to Army H.Q. and supplement my observations of the traffic on the new line with a verbal report. They had been waiting for this information for a very long time.

Our gale flight had proved remunerative.

CHAPTER VIII

GOOD SHOT!

WE were equipped with telescopic sights for our bombing operations. Even a novice could plant his eggs well on the mark with the aid of this metre-long instrument. But thirty kilometres the other side of the lines it was likely to fare ill with anyone who pressed his eye to the eyepiece for even a minute instead of using it to search the sky for enemy aircraft. We therefore did not carry out the instruction: "Telescopic sight to be always used for bombing operations" in its true sense. We dropped our bombs with the aid of the naked eye, while the telescopic sight remained at rest in its tough cardboard case; the main thing was that we had it actually "with" us.

Later on these stately instruments wandered secretly to the stores.

A pleasant rest to them there!

. . . . .

Orders: The usual long distance reconnaissance. One incendiary and four explosive bombs on Epernay.

We cross the front happily to the north-west of Rheims, worming in half-way between two anti-aircraft batteries. As their positions are fairly wide apart, their bursts can hardly reach us. To our hearty delight several shells burst a good two kilometres away from us.

We reach Epernay *via* the Rheims Wood. As the wind in these parts is blowing straight from the south, we are unfortunately prevented from sailing down the length of the line, and must cross it instead. I therefore have very little room to work in, and must take accurate aim.

The first Archie shells burst a happy distance away, so that we need not go into any turns on their account.

Engmann flies on to the mark in irreproachable fashion. A few more seconds—then we'll have the right position—hand on lever—now—go!

But unfortunately the cold plays me a dirty trick. Despite their double casing of a silk glove and a leather one lined with fur my fingers have grown so stiff that there is no feeling left in them. They pull the lever too far, and the explosive bombs drop out in a bunch instead of one by one. I gaze after them with some slight regret. Then I sent the incendiary bomb after them and wait for the result.

If I have aimed correctly, the massed drop will give a fourfold good result. But if I have missed the mark, all four will be wasted.

However my luck has not deserted me, for it has delivered my parcel right on top of the huge sheds. A thick trail of smoke curls up from the roof.

Soon afterwards the incendiary bomb announces its presence. It goes down on the tracks leading into a shed, from which bright flames break out a little while afterwards.

With a joyful heart I tell Engmann the good news. His eyes reflect it, and he laughs as he points downwards. An engine-driver has got the wind up and hustles his train out of the way. The engine emits thick clouds of steam, which give wonderful plastic effects against the dark background in the cold air. Now the train is passing under the bridge that carries the road—the white steam is broken off—only to rise again mightily on the farther side of the bridge.

I cannot help thinking of Chamisso's poem, "The Giant's Toy." I too am glad to have brought so much trouble on the little children of earth down there.

Onward to St. Hilaire!

The Archies at the railway triangle intend to puff us up a warm welcome. They succeed—as far as its quantity is concerned—but happily the road made by the shellbursts lies a good 1,000 metres behind our line of flight. Nevertheless we go into a few small turns, so as to keep the gunners firing at a wrong elevation, and the poor dears are so credulous!

GOOD SHOT!

Suddenly Engmann chirps away with his throttle: "Trrrp! Trrrp! Trrrp!"

I turn round—a Caudron is advancing towards us! (Photograph 10.)

I stare after him as he flits away several hundred metres below us and pull my machine-gun round. As soon as he turns, I shall strew my morning blessings on his head. But he is so busy looking for us in his line of flight that he fails to notice us here—just one storey up. He flies straight for the Archie cloudlets floating behind us in the air.

While I am considering whether an attack is worth while, I am presented with a wonderful surprise packet. The Archies from which we have just escaped imagine we have turned back and so put a murderous fire on to their compatriot. Moreover their bursts which were too low for us are just the right elevation for the Caudron flying at a lower level.

We fly home full of malicious glee.

CHAPTER IX

SPÄTZLE

CAPTAIN Hans Linke (pilot) and Lieutenant Steinbrenner (observer) had trained into a splendid team and thought that nothing but peace could part them. But " the airman proposes, the Kogenluft[1] disposes."

When Captain " Hänschen " got a fighting Staffel on the Somme front, Lieutenant Spätzle could only wait until his former pilot had a vacancy and could

[1] Kogenluft = Kommandierender General der Luftstreitkräfte, (General commanding the fighting air forces.)

SPÄTZLE

put in for him. Meanwhile he was allotted to Lieutenant Laucke.

. . . . .

A hard bang at the door startles me out of my dreams. I sit up sleepily. Ah, yes, I'm due to issue the bombs. I open the window and look out. Before my dwelling stands the car, with Steinbrenner and Laucke.

"Morning! I'll be down in a moment!"

Boots on—cap on—overcoat over pyjamas—down stairs.

A wonderful May morning; birds singing in the garden. Spätzle follows my looks.

"What's the good of their pretty little chirps to me when I've got to take bombs up?" he remarks.

"Another 50-kilo like the one you put on Heinrich's brewery?"

He laughs and disclaims any desire for it. "I haven't 50 pfennigs' worth of bombing ambition inside me. I'd much prefer to leave them all at home. But what can you do when you get your orders? So in God's name give me a 50 fellow. Then at least I'll get rid of the muck at one fell swoop."

. . . . .

They take off at 5.30 a.m.

Steinbrenner is in a bad temper. After a full hour's flying the machine has only climbed to a miserable 2,700 metres. With a hundredweight of bomb ballast on board it is not likely to go much higher in this air that carries it so badly—so better make straight for the lines!

While they cross the front at Massiges, some other folk behind the lines are stirring up the witches' cauldron into which they will blunder unawares. The fighting squadron has mustered its Staffels for a bombing raid on the plant of the Noblette-Auve valley railway and Suippes aerodrome. The French squadrons have taken off to repel them, and Laucke is steering right into this swarm of hornets.

Not a cloud in the sky. There are only just a few shreds of milk-white ground-mist left clinging to the trees of the Argonne Wood. The day promises fair. The Archies at the front content themselves with a few perfunctory rounds. Steinbrenner peers out. Four machines hang in the air five kilometres to the southward of him, but as they are flying considerably higher, he can sneak past them.

Laucke follow the Ménehould-Suippes line. Not a Frenchman to be seen anywhere; they seem to have dodged through successfully. Seem, yes, but when Steinbrenner is about to take a photograph over Somme-Suippes, he catches sight of the first Caudron making for him.

Away with the camera—down with the bombs any old where—round with the machine-gun.

Meanwhile the Frenchman has climbed to 500 metres above him and goes into a slanting dive from behind.

Tacktacktacktacktack!

The Frenchman turns away from the burst, leaving a free target for the second Caudron, who promptly hammers away.

As the enemy has come out of the sun, Steinbrenner

SPÄTZLE

whacks his pilot back to the front. While he is still firing at the Caudron, another burst hails down on him most surprisingly from above and to one side—a Spad! And somewhat farther back there is yet another one whirling up.

Steinbrenner is kneeling as he shoots. Suddenly he finds he cannot keep his position, because the machine has gone down on her nose. He looks in front of him—Laucke crouches hunched up over the stick. A red stream courses down his back—shot through the neck. It means the finish for both of them if he loses consciousness from loss of blood, and yet it is impossible to give him an emergency dressing during the fight.

The heavy pressure on the stick puts the machine down to such an extent that the Frenchmen disappear under the wings and only come into view every now and then. They can put their bursts into the target again and again without interference.

Just as a Spad comes into Steinbrenner's sights at last, something hits his left foot hard. Another blow follows hard upon it—blood gushes from his boot— two shots in the foot!

Another burst rattles into the machine. Wood cracks—metal screeches—good shot! The next moment the manometer's hand begins to fall—tank holed. The propeller goes slower and slower— flutters round a few more times—and goes dead.

Again and again Steinbrenner strives to get a sight on to the enemy firing from safe cover. The last of the 250 cartridges in the first drum has just gone before a bullet hits it.

New drum! It is hit before he can fix it to the machine-gun. Away with it, and on with the last drum!

The change wastes precious seconds. But—what luck!—the two Caudrons are sheering off. And now one of the Spads goes into a banked turn that brings him right on to his wing-tips.

Steinbrenner draws a deep breath. Now he has only one opponent to deal with. But the latter must have noticed the dead prop and be preparing to give the Boche his *coup de grâce*.

A look overboard. Barely a thousand metres up, but over the French lines. If Laucke can stick it, there is perhaps a chance of getting out of the horrible mess.

Just as Steinbrenner is about to shoot again, the last opponent goes into a turn.

Saved—if the pilot can hold out!

And he does hold out.

The wounded bird slides down between the barbed wire entanglements of the reserve positions and makes a good landing on a fallow field. A rise ahead covers it from the enemy's ground observations. Infantrymen rush up and lift the two wounded men out. While Laucke is being carried to a dressing station, Steinbrenner directs them to roll the machine back until a steep slope conceals it from the enemy's air observation and covers it from shrapnel fire. Only when this is done does he permit himself to be conveyed to the dressing station.

His foresight is rewarded. A few minutes later the French captive balloon on the other side goes up to spy out the machine that made a forced landing and put the artillery on to it.

Just a little bit too late!

. . . . .

I fetched our two wounded friends in a car and delivered them to the field hospital; I also saw the machine brought back. (Photograph 11.) A few days afterwards we were able to give Spätzle a piece of good news; his transfer to Linke's fighting Staffel was arranged.

Despite the cumbrous plaster dressing he was in good spirits—and doubly so when he received our tidings. (Photograph 12.)

His comradeship with Linke endured till death. Their machine was shot down over Vaux Wood and destroyed by shellfire, along with its crew.

CHAPTER X

A PAINFUL PREDICAMENT

RETURNING from Rethel one evening, Holzhausen and Hörnig brought good news with them.
" Our fighting squadron has been withdrawn ! "
Its presence had burdened us with a number of extra French Archies and scouts. As its huge mach-

A PAINFUL PREDICAMENT

ines (photograph 13) only bombed objectives that lay outside the artillery range, its field of action coincided with our reconnaissance area. A wasps' nest was stirred up on the other side, but the stirrers did not get the stings.

They were reserved for the passers-by—i.e., the airmen of Flying Section 17.

. . . . .

Unfortunately Captain Mohr poured water into the wine of our delight a few days later.

To prevent the French getting too uppish after the withdrawal of our fighting squadron all aircraft attached to this army corps are to undertake collective bombing raids every now and then. They are going to issue us those torpedo-shaped PuW. bombs, which create a far better effect than our old pears. He turned to me. "You're for the park to-morrow, to take over the new bombing apparatus, with which all machines are to be fitted at once."

. . . . .

Three days later eighteen machines went up to take part in the first squadron exercises. We mustered at Lessingcourt, each machine carrying two $12\frac{1}{2}$-kilo bombs.

After the three Staffels had assembled in the air above their own territory—A over Lessincourt village, B over the "Spider's web" crossroads, C over the manœuvre ground—a T landing mark was put out and a Very light went up. Thereupon each Staffel formed up, with all its six machines flying in a line, 100 metres apart.

The squadron-leader fired another Very light, which

each of the Staffel-leaders had to answer. This was the signal to start.

Our bombing practice-ground at Pauvres represented the objective. It was laid out with skeleton railway sidings and sheds, and even two wooden dummy machines.

A third Very light: left turn all machines—form up in column—down to 1,500 metres—fly on target—drop bombs—fly back to home aerodrome.

. . . . .

Everything goes off fairly well until after the discharge of the second Very light. The machines of No. 17—following instructions—drop down to 1,500 metres and fly on the target.

I look round for the other Staffels. One is flying in front of us, but the other—and here my nerves receive a mild shock—is right over our heads. As they are flying on the same target as ourselves, we are directly below them. I stare up at them in rage. If they should drop their bombs now, chance might ordain that these blessings descend upon our heads.

Engmann has also noticed the threatening danger and grows restless. I have to quieten him down with a love-tap and then whack him on to the target. As the new bomb-racks are fitted underneath the machines, it is easier for the pilot to release the safety catches on the holders than the observer. I bend over to Engmann and remind him: "Release!" He nods his "O.K." and gropes for the lever behind him with his left hand.

I sight the target and pull.

"Ruck! Ruck!"

A PAINFUL PREDICAMENT 63

A second later I see two steel fish whirl through the air on our right; they are almost near enough for me to touch as they pass. The gentleman on the floor above us has also dropped his packet. Mercifully it has passed us by.

I cannot note where our bombs have fallen because the ground is thick with the dirt thrown up by the others. So back to Attigny!

With tender pressure on his shoulders I give Engmann instructions to go into a left-hand turn and am just about to sit down on my tip-up seat once more. Suddenly my glance turns to the hole in the floor and freezes—there is a bomb still hanging in the rack. As Engmann released the safety catches, it must have jammed and may fall any moment. It will fall on our own territory, perhaps in the very midst of the comrades who are staring up at us in curiosity.

I bend over to Take and make him cut his engine. " Fly on the target again; there's a bomb still hanging there."

At once Engmann grabs instinctively at the safety catch. Oh damn, in the fluster caused by the danger threatening from above he released only one bomb! Now he quickly frees the other one—and as I have previously pulled my lever to drop both bombs, the torpedo whirls down earthwards the very next moment.

I feel as if all the roots of my hair are on fire.

I look down. Our turn has already taken us out of the fenced-off area. Close before us lies the hill on which the spectators of the operations have assembled on account of the good view it gives them. They include not merely our section-commander and Captain Drechsel, the O.C. Aviation, but also Colonel Baron von Olderhausen, the chief of the 3rd Army's staff.

I cannot see the hit yet. A dud, perhaps? No—there's a flash down below—followed at once by a great cloud of smoke and dust. The bomb has burst hard by the hill where the bigwigs are standing.

My limbs freeze to ice. Then I become a fatalist. What is done cannot be undone—not all the good will in the world can alter by a hair's breadth the consequences of Take's unlucky action.

But Engmann seems to have lost his wits. He crouches over his stick, glancing neither to right nor left. The few minutes of our flight to Attigny expand into hours. If only we knew what that bomb has done!

When we have landed, Engmann's eyes are big with terror as he tries to stammer out his explanations. I point to the squad of mechanics hastening up and put my finger on my lips: "Afterwards!"

Meanwhile our other five machines come humming down. Their crews are boastfully happy at having the unpopular trial squadron-flight behind them. They pile themselves quickly into the cars waiting to take them to the town.

"Aren't you coming along?" someone asks.

I decline. "No, thanks, we'd rather walk."

When the cars have gone, we stroll off behind them.

"Take!"

He is all in pieces.

"Herr Lieutenant—I don't know how it happened—I didn't think what I was doing—I only wanted to put my mistake right and—and——"

11. Spätzle's Machine after a Fight.

12. 'Spätzle in Hospital.'

A PAINFUL PREDICAMENT

I shrug my shoulders in resignation. "Take, that will cost us our jobs and our wings—the Kofl—the chief of the staff——"

Engmann pulls up suddenly. "If anything has happened, I'll put a bullet through my head. I can't stick the disgrace."

I try to comfort him, but he shakes his head sadly.

In the mess I find all the others in a boisterous mood, except Holzhausen and Beckmann, who are having a violent argument. Their machines nearly collided in the air, but neither will take the blame.

I conceal my depression and join in the general laughter. All the time my heart is tortured with the maddening uncertainty. I still have one faint hope—no one has rung up.

At last, after half an hour, a car arrives. A few moments later Captain Mohr enters the room with a gloomy face. The officers are hungry and look forward pleasurably to the evening meal, but the captain summons us to a conference and sends for all the N.C.O. pilots.

"Some unlucky blighter has dropped a bomb close to the observation post—happily without doing any damage."

He scans us with the sharp eyes of a detective. I make the same expectant face as the others—but it is only a mask. My heart sings a joyful song: "Take, dear old Take, it's all right now!"

I dare not look at him for fear of giving ourselves away. Not until the N.C.O.s file out can I answer his side-glance by half closing my left eye.

The language of gaol-birds.

E

CHAPTER XI

THE SQUADRON FLIGHT

A few days after our trial raid orders reached us from G.H.Q.:

"Squadron bomb raid by machines 3rd Army on Revigny station to assist operations Verdun front."

. . . . .

My batman rouses me a few hours after midnight. As we have flown our machines to Lessincourt aerodrome the day before, a motor-bus is waiting to take us there.

A starless night. The heavy mist makes the darkness still thicker. Our squadron commander is therefore still in two minds: to be or not to be? The

THE SQUADRON FLIGHT 67

old hands can find their way there and back, of course —but what about the greenhorns? Resolution: leave the final decision until after the machines have started, because it will be easier to judge the weather from up aloft than down on the grass.

Once more our instructions are repeated to us. Climb up over the same area as in the trial. If the commander decides to call the raid off, he will fire two fog-shells as a landing signal. If this signal is not forthcoming, Staffel-leaders will fire a white and a green light at 4.15. a.m. as an order to their machines to go ahead.

All clear. The contrasts of light and shade on the aerodrome form a fantastic nocturne. Broad ribbons of light from the illuminated sheds and huts course across the grass, while the flashes of electric torches flit like glow-worms over the ground. Here and there a tiny point of light pulls the cockpit or wings of some machine out of the darkness. Blue jets of flame spurt from the exhaust valves.

The roar from the trial runs of the engines is such that one can hardly hear one's own voice.

Order is brought into this anthill as soon as the landing lights are lit. The mechanics wheel their machines carefully to the end of the aerodrome, so as to avoid all danger of collisions on the ground, and then we take off at one minute intervals.

Now it is our turn. As soon as I have strapped myself in, we taxi off. Two flares at the "Spider's Web" mark our mustering place. The aerodrome and its lights are well behind us.

As it would be easy to collide with some comrade

here, we climb away to one side. The flares and coloured lights are easy to see.

. . . . .

4.15 a.m.

Where are those light signals? Have we missed them? Have the others started off? Engmann throttles down.

"No signal! Land?"

"No! Don't want to look fools by being the only ones to land. Nothing doing. Make for the lines!" Engmann obediently opens his throttle and steers a southerly course.

Lo—from the aerodrome a fiery serpent shoots up cometwise to us—a second one follows it—and the night's blackness is rent by two livid flashes. A good thing that we have a signal—and mean of them to send a landing one.

Engmann promptly goes into a glide. I grab him by the neck. "Engine full till I give orders to go down!"

He nods and pushes his throttle-lever forward again. I give vent to a doleful grunt. Why should we land? The weather could not be better for us; darkness and mist are just what we want.

We are flying! I bend over to Engmann and shout against the roar of the engine into his ear:

"Rrre—vig—nyyy!"

He nods and makes straight for the front. Then something unexpected occurs to change my bad mood into vainglorious mirth—to our left green and white lights shoot up out of the air. It is the attack signal, given by Casparito who leads our Staffel.

13. Large Machine belonging to the German Fighter Squadron.

14. Remains of the Machine Berger destroyed after Landing.

Order—counter order—disorder!

I have to laugh heartily. Now no one knows what we are supposed to do. The fog-shell says "Land," and the lights say "Go ahead." So we can all do what we like. A lovely mess-up!

Meanwhile a faint glow has broken out somewhere about east-north-east.

The coming day is on us.

We cross the lines at Massiges. Our positions on the hill there that push themselves into the enemy like a nose are unrecognizable. I have chosen this far westerly route so that the batteries at Ste Ménehould cannot reach us afterwards. If I can carry out my job without obstruction by enemy Archies or aircraft, it is not valour but sheer stupidity to charge into the thick of them.

The Archies at the front do not waste even a single shot in trying to scare us. But heavy fire flashes up from the direction of Vienne-le-Château. I shake my head. Why must our people cross just there where it fairly bristles with batteries? Their own fault! But when I put my glasses to my eyes I let them fall again with a smile of satisfaction; those are not Archies, but the heavy guns north-west of Verdun.

The faint south-westerly wind does not push us much off our course. I am agreeably surprised at our good progress; in the darkness and mist I feel as small and insignificant as the needle in the proverbial haystack.

I whack Engmann into a south-east course when we have snaked our way past Ste Ménehould and its Archies. The circle of light, which the rising sun has enlarged considerably, is reflected on the two big lakes embedded in the Argonne forest. A reference to the map shows me that we are not far from Revigny.

I crane my neck forward. Over yonder the railway, which we must fly along, flows into a huge station—our target!

I let Engmann keep the dumps on his right so that the south-west breeze can carry our torpedoes on to the target. So—good! I despatch the bombs at intervals of a few seconds.

Not one Archie cloudlet high or low, not a machine anywhere in the sky. I turn my eyes to the ground to watch for the hits. Ah, a flash down below!

No 1 : on an open field—oh hell!

No 2 : a bit nearer—hopeful.

No 3 : in the big dumps to north of the station —*bon jour, messieurs.*

No 4 : right between the lines—hurrah!

We buzz off contentedly north-eastwards so as to cut through south of Verdun. The French are expecting us to go home via Ste Ménehould and will hardly bother about us round St Mihiel. Moreover, this course gives us the south-west breeze on our backs.

Suddenly I give a nervous start. Engmann has chirped his throttle three times : enemy aircraft. I cannot make out the type. Round with the machine-gun!

The machine is on us in an instant, and flits past us. But—it carries crosses, not cockades—a friend. While I am staring after it, the first explosions flame up into the sea of mist. Probably the bulk of our squadron has turned up to lay its eggs. We who are already buzzing off are too insignificant for further notice. And that is not at all displeasing, because the Revigny Archies are known to be nasty fellows. Ten weeks ago they brought Lieutenant von Pappritz's Zeppelin down in flames.

Turning round, I see another machine humming along. A Frenchman! A Voisin—can't possibly mistake his front elevator. He whizzes past us at barely 200 metres distance. Now he will turn and take us on—no, he flies onward! The Napoleonic principle—always make for the thunder of the guns—therefore applies to air fights in only a limited measure; it is so easy to overlook the good things that fly by so close at hand.

Below me, to the right, lies Bar-le-Duc, nestling between wooded heights. A few days ago the Nieuport squadron there shot down the leading machine of our Fighting Staffel 4, which carried Captain Detten.

Having searched the air for enemies, I note the railway traffic on my map. It is very lively on the stretch between Revigny and Verdun.

In the far distance I see the Meuse valley, where morning mists are ascending. On the heights beyond massed clusters of artillery flashes and shellbursts are visible.

Engmann's hand points to our right. Another doubledecker! But as he goes into a turn, I lay my machine-gun to rest. A German! And now Archie cloudlets shoot up—and again—more and more of them. But they are all after the machine that has just turned away from us; not one shell comes near us. As we are flying out of their hinterland, the French gunners take us for a *camarade*.

The feelings within me are mixed ones. I am sorry to see our friend get such a peppering—but likewise glad that we are left alone. As in the well-known peasant's prayer:

> St. Florian, spare my house, I pray,
> And burn some other man's to-day.

But retribution is already on the way. When across the Meuse we get a warm basting from the Archies of the front. The first shells put the wind up us—their detonations are so loud that there is no mistake about their nearness. We get out of their fire, however, by a steep dive.

Down on the left lies Verdun. Shells are falling there; several houses are in flames.

The front lies buried beneath thick clouds of smoke and dirt, through which only the bright flashes of the guns are visible. A feeling of respect for our bleeding comrades down there takes possession of us as we fly over it.

Then we head northwards. For the moment we keep behind the German lines, excepting for a cut across the north-east edge of the front. Beneath our feet lie the fiercely contested forts, Vaux and Douamont. Vaux is not to be seen; a hurricane of fire and smoke veils it from our view.

We bend off to north-west. The front, with all its terrific impressions, lies ever farther and farther behind us. When we have crossed the Argonne woods, we follow the line of the peaceful Aisne valley and land in Lessincourt about 8.20 a.m.

The results of our squadron flight are meagre

THE SQUADRON FLIGHT 73

enough. Eleven of the eighteen machines concerned landed in response to the signal of the fog-shell; they were lucky to escape with only one crash. One of the seven that followed the signal of the green and white lights to go ahead lost the way completely and made a forced landing in some distant parts—luckily on German territory. Six machines, i.e., one third of the original force, unloaded their bombs on Revigny—and of these six, four belonged to Flying Section 17.

CHAPTER XII

SHOT DOWN

LATE in the afternoon I had to take an extensive airing. I flew a barrage patrol over Attigny station, where the Grand Duke of Mecklenburg-Schwerin had arrived on a visit to his troops. When I came into the mess that evening, I stopped in the corridor and listened in some surprise. Yes, I ought to know that gay laugh! I entered, full of curiosity—and found Berger had really come back!

The bone wound and the ten flesh ones he had received on his virgin flight fifteen weeks ago had all healed well. He was as sprightly again as a May morning and thirsted for fresh deeds.

"So to-morrow afternoon I'll repeat my virgin flight with Schattat," he announced.

We had to inform him:

"Virgin flights cannot be made twice. In case of need we're ready to allow a demi-vierge flight."

Captain Wolff nodded.

"Or we might nominate you an honorary virgin—Latin :—virgo honoris causa."

. . . . .

While we were seated at dinner the following night the orderly came in and lit up. I felt somewhat depressed.

"Berger and Schattat not back yet?"

Captain Mohr consoled me. "They didn't take off till just after six."

I stared out of the window. It had grown quite dark. There—the drone of an engine. We breathed sighs of relief.

"Our little ace is coming along!"

A few minutes afterwards the aerodrome squad telephoned to report the landing, and a quarter of an hour later Berger entered the room with a beaming face.

"Well, my little lad, you come with such a victorious countenance that we'd like to congratulate you in advance. What's your good news? Shot anything down? Discovered a new French aerodrome?"

With a cheerful smile Berger reported himself to the captain.

"Unfortunately we did not reach the lines on

account of a strong headwind and nightfall. Flight broken off over Warmeriville."

We laughed till the tears ran out of our eyes. We should have probably done the same thing—but one had the feeling that Providence had intervened on Berger's behalf.

His laughter was the heartiest of all. " Boys, I'll do it yet. I'll take on any bet you like that I'll reach Châlons to-morrow."

Although we pulled his leg severely that evening, his imperturbable placidity and confidence in victory made an impression on us. Captain Mohr nodded.

" Yes, you'll have to do it to-morrow. And so as to give you every chance I'll put you with Sergeant Stattaus, who is one of my best pilots."

Beaming with joy, Berger thanked him.

. . . . .

When I strolled home from the mess I saw a light in Stattaus' quarters. I looked through the window into the room—he was writing. Every now and then he turned over the pages of some book.

I had made my first front-flights with Stattaus and felt a great liking for this redheaded East Prussian. So I knocked and entered.

" Well, Stattaus, didn't they teach you spelling at school? Else why do you have to look up almost every word?"

Stattaus had risen and was standing before me with a blushing face.

" No, Herr Lieutenant; it's a French letter, and I'm getting the right expressions out of the dictionary."

I had to laugh.

15. BERGER AND STATTAUS, WITH THE FRENCH COMMANDANT.

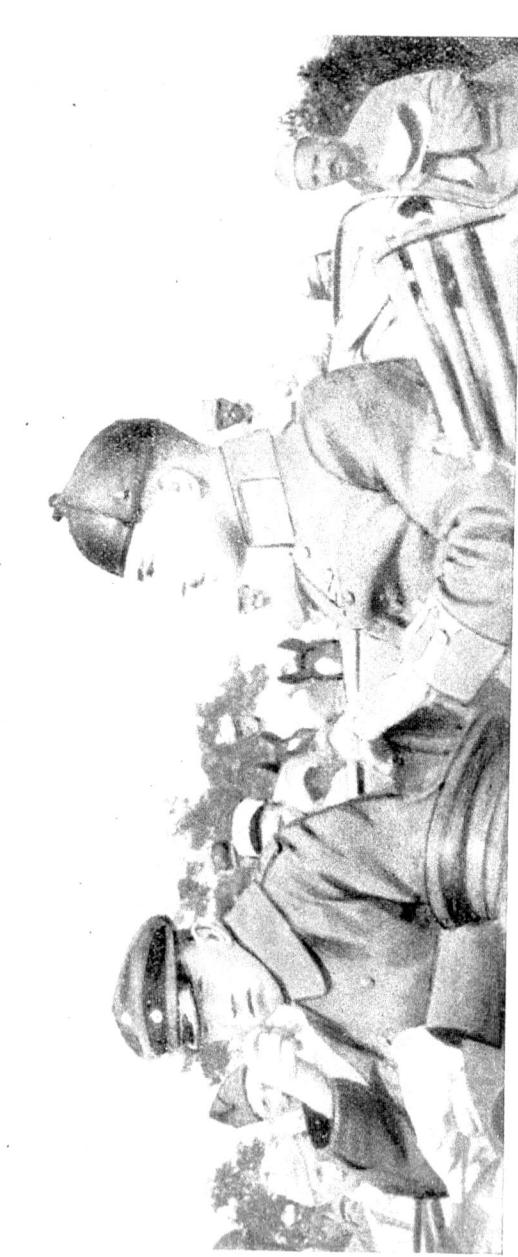

16. Stattaus and Berger on the way to their Examination.

" That means a love-letter. But, man alive, you don't need to blush for it. Shall I translate it for you ? " But when he declined with some embarrassment, I began to realize that one can never be of any assistance in affairs of the heart.

" Well, then try to get through it yourself," I said. " As love is international, you will surely be able to make yourself understood. But remember that ' kiss ' is not ' baiser ' in French, but ' embrasser.' I hope you'll get it finished by to-morrow morning."

Stattaus shook his head. " I'm nearly down to the end of the paper. Besides, I'll have to go to bed soon, because I'm on the first patrol to-morrow with Herr Lieutenant Berger."

" Oh yes. What's the job ? "

He showed me his map. " Usual long distance reconnaissance. With photographs of Oiry and Châlons stations, and Auve, La Cheppe, Valmy and Ménehould aerodromes."

"Well, there are quite a nice lot of clouds in the sky, so that you'll be able to have your sleep out all the same. Good night—and sweet dreams of her ! "

. . . . .

The next day we were assembled in the mess for lunch, and only waiting for our leader. But when at length he arrived, his curt greeting foreboded ill news.

" Berger and Stattaus overdue."

We stared at one another in consternation. Was Berger in for a third stroke of bad luck ?

" When did they start ? "

" 8 a.m. And it's now 12.30."

Boormann still had faint hopes. " There was a

north wester of thirty metres a second up aloft this morning. Perhaps they used it to take them over the lines somewhere south of Verdun."

. . . . .

When the skipper visited me on the aerodrome that afternoon, his confidence had sunk to zero.

"I rang up the Crown Prince Kofl. No machine landed round there. So they're missing, and I'll have to ask you to take their job on. Take off at 5 p.m."

Despite our low spirits we could not help laughing. A strange coincidence had ordained that I should finish Berger's interrupted job for him to-day, just as I had done when he was first shot down.

But this time it was not to be. The clouds gathered together, and a couple of heavy thunderstorms hung over the front. I was unable to glean the aftermath.

. . . . .

But what had happened to our comrades?

Not a shot was fired when they crossed the lines above a heavy cloudbank over Rheims.

On to Châlons!

They made good progress with a favouring wind behind them. Not a sign of any enemy aircraft.

But the gunners heard the drone of our machine and put up a heavy barrage. It did not impress Stattaus; often enough he had needs must worm through the shellbursts round Châlons way! Besides, the shells were bursting about 1,000 metres too low.

There was a pause in the fire for a whole minute. Then came thunder and lightning from a clear sky! a deafening detonation! The very first shell fired at the new range had burst close under their machine.

When Stattaus saw the rev.-counter dropping quickly, he turned straight back for the lines.

A rain of sparks and a strong smell of petrol—radiator and gravity tank holed—the leads of the main tank shattered. The engine gets no more fuel and goes dead.

Will they cross the lines with this strong headwind against them?

Is their password to be " Home " or " P.G. "?[1]

They are still 4,800 metres up, but the slender hand of the rev.-counter goes back inexorably. 4,700 . . . 4,600 . . . 4,500 . . .

As the engine has stopped roaring, the detonations sound unpleasantly loud in their ears. The gunners below have seen their success; they start a veritable quick-fire. Shells and shrapnel screech incessantly. Often they come threateningly near, forcing Stattaus into turns. With a dead engine these mean loss of height and direction.

Lieutenant Berger leans over anxiously. " Shall we do it ? "

Stattaus shrugs his shoulders. " Hope so, Herr Lieutenant." He tries every possible trick to make his glide as flat as possible and prolong his progress. But the strong north-wester beats mercilessly against the machine, so that its forward movement is infinitely slow.

Berger throws overboard everything that is not indispensable. He smashes his plates and sends them down; then the camera follows after he has broken the lens and shutter. Two drums of ammunition whirl

[1] P.G. = Prisonnier de Guerre (Prisoner of War).

after them; he keeps only the machine-gun and the third drum.

Deeper and deeper they glide; ever more painful is the certainty that gnaws at their hearts—captivity.

They flit past a captive balloon at 700 metres. Impossible to reach the trenches now! But all the same Stattaus heads an obstinate course for the lines. In the depths of his heart he still believes in miracles.

300 metres above ground. The chalk thrown up by the German positions looks almost near enough to touch; comrades stare up with troubled eyes from them.

Berger thinks it out—a Very light in the main tank as soon as they land—it is to be hoped it is not quite dry, so that he can start a decent blaze. "The machine must be destroyed, even at the risk of your own life." How often have those instructions been hammered into him!

100 metres.

Yonder, near the pine woods—a fallow field.

Stattaus pushes the stick down hard and goes full tilt at it. He hopes to shave off the undercarriage with a rough landing.

But, as usual, things do not happen as they should. The thick rubber layers that act as springs to the axle absorb the shock elastically and throw the machine up in the air again. Down goes the stick once more—the machine makes a good landing and taxies on cleanly.

The two men jump out before it comes to a standstill. From a couple of metres away Berger fires his Very pistol with the magnesium bullets into the main

SHOT DOWN

tank—a few seconds later the machine blazes up like a torch.

They have landed close to a battery position. The gunners come rushing from their dug-outs in the pine wood and level their carbines at the Germans. When they see the latter are unarmed, they approach, laughing.

"*Ah, boche capoutte!*"

While some chat with Berger, others hasten to the machine. Fearful lest they should put the blaze out, Stattaus holds them back.

"Nix, Mossoo, bumm, bumm! Mossoo caput!"

The Frenchmen heed his warning and keep a respectful distance. (Photograph 14.)

The next moment the drone of an engine is heard in the air, and a Nieuport lands a minute later. The officer-pilot jumps out and rushes to the burning machine. When he sees there is no hope of saving it, he shrugs his shoulders and goes up to Lieutenant Berger, speaking in fluent German:

"Good day, comrade. You have had bad luck. All the same I must congratulate you on having destroyed your machine. Sad as this may be for us, it will be a source of proud satisfaction for you."

This compliment from the enemy's mouth cheers Berger up somewhat.

Soon afterwards a car containing officers of the French Air Force hastens up. The first series of questions begins. Our two decline to make any statements on military matters. Then Lieutenant Berger addresses the French section-commander. (Photograph 15.)

F

"I have one request. Please drop a message behind our lines, saying that we were shot down by anti-aircraft fire, but neither of us was wounded, and we were taken prisoners after setting fire to our machine."

· · · · ·

Not long afterwards the French actually fulfilled this request. But before they did so, we learnt the consoling certainty that our comrades were unhurt through a paragraph in the *Figaro*, which I took in *via* Switzerland:

FIGHTING IN THE AIR
ON THE FRENCH FRONT

In the Champagne an Aviatik that had been badly hit in a fight in the air fell behind its own lines to the north of Somme-Py. Another enemy aeroplane was hit by our anti-aircraft batteries and forced to land north-east of Somme-Suippes. Its two inmates were taken prisoners.

· · · · ·

When the French realized that they could get no information out of our people, they conveyed them by car to Hans, where they were due to submit to another cross-fire of questions at H.Q. (Photograph 16.) Stattaus sat in his corner with a grim face, but when he tried to pull his handkerchief out of his flying-jacket, he gave a start of dismay. The pocket still contained his letter to the little French girl! How embarrassing if it should chance to be discovered by his captors!

So he resolved to destroy it.

A poilu with a loaded rifle sat next to the driver.

He only turned back to look at the prisoners every now and then. He knew they could not jump out of a car travelling at such a pace.

Stattaus has made up his mind. He tears the letter in pieces in his pocket. When his guard is looking straight ahead he puts his clenched fist over the side of the car and opens it. Bad luck! The wind carries the fragments forward and whirls them on to the guard's nose. The latter bids the driver stop. With an angry face he points to his rifle and makes threatening gestures at Stattaus. Then he gathers all the bits and pieces and puts them in his pocket.

. . . . .

The Army H.Q. at Hans village.

An examination of all pockets. Nothing found!

" What was in the report which you tore to pieces?"

" That was a private letter!"

" We'll see."

Two officers of the general staff cross-examine Berger and Stattaus.

" Is there an aerodrome at Monthois?"

" We don't know."

" Where is your Flying Section 17 stationed?"

" We are not allowed to say."

" How many sections are there in the Champagne?"

" Where is your army's aircraft park?" " Are you getting adequate replacements from Germany?"

" How many Fokker Staffels are there in the Champagne?"

The reply is always the same: " We are not allowed to say."

The examination is over. The two prisoners are led off separately. They will not meet again until many years afterwards, in Breslau.

. . . . .

When Stattaus is brought before the staff officers a second time, they receive him with laughter.

"There are evidently some nice girls in Attigny for the flying men of Section 17?"

Stattaus is as embarrassed as a schoolboy when they thrust the love-letter—carefully pasted together—under his nose. Luckily several scraps of it were carried away by a gust of wind.

"What's the little girl's name?"

Stattaus remains a perfect gentleman and refuses to answer. Then when the cross-examination about military matters recommences he takes refuge in obstinate silence. One of the officers, a certain Captain Hagen, gives the conversation a personal twist:

"I studied at Leipzig once, and afterwards I made the acquaintance of a Captain Göbel in Paris. Please give him my greetings if you should happen to see him after the war."

Then he gently slides over to military questions once more. When he gets no results, he tries to trap Stattaus by showing him photographs of German aerodromes taken from the air.

"Look here, this is your Section 10's aerodrome, isn't it?"

As once again no answer can be extracted from him, the Frenchmen grow ungracious.

"We'll find means to make you talkative!"

Stattaus is led away.

. . . . .

He sinks down wearily on the straw in his cell. But the day's impressions are so overpowering that they will not let him sleep.

"Really I behaved like an idiot. Of course one shouldn't land behind the lines where the ground is thick with the enemy; one should pick out a spot in the hinterland where there aren't so many people about. Then you climb out, burn your machine and hide yourself. A French machine is sure to land in the neighbourhood. As soon as the pilot gets out and goes to look at the blaze, I can sneak up to his machine, jump in and buzz off. But those are lost chances, my lad.

"If only—if only—if only——"

"I shan't get away from here so easily. The windows are heavily barred, and outside there's a sentinel with a loaded rifle. No use thinking of escaping!"

For the present, at least!

. . . . .

Stattaus rouses himself with a start from dismal dreams.

In the pale morning light he recognizes the sentinel, who stands before him with fixed bayonet and shakes his arm. Still drunk with sleep, he rises and files out before the soldier. Outside a car is waiting to bear him swiftly to Châlons.

They reach the town in half an hour. He is driven slowly through the streets on which he has so often gazed down from aloft. Inquisitive, maliciously exultant civilians and soldiers stare at the captive Boche airman. The car halts before a large building, the barred windows of which leave no doubt as to its use. Stattaus is led up steps and along narrow corridors. The warder opens a door and thrusts him in. Stattaus cannot yet understand this treatment.

"*Pourquoi?*" he asks.

"Twenty-one days cells for refusing to answer questions."

The heavy door is slammed to with a bang.

CHAPTER XIII

HONOURING A HERO

AND how fares it with Berger?
He is separated from Stattaus after the first examination and shut up in a small hut. When he looks out of the window after a brief nap, he cannot help laughing in spite of all his tribulations, for meanwhile a dense barbed wire entanglement has grown up around his villa secretly, silently, and stealthily.

. . . . . .

He receives a pleasant surprise on his return from his second examination. With comradely solicitude for his welfare the French airmen have not only provided him with rugs and books; they have even sent him food and cigarettes as well.

* * * * *

A day or two afterwards they send a car to bring him to their aerodrome, where they give him a most friendly welcome. Berger knows that their action is not prompted by pure lovingkindness; they would like to extract some information on military matters as well. But all the same he finds it quite pleasant. They make light of his gratitude.

"We work on the same principles as you do: man to man when we meet in the air—gentleman to gentleman when we meet on the ground. And in addition we feel particularly happy in being able to welcome to our midst one of the famous German aces."

Berger feels somewhat annoyed to find himself even here twitted with his bad luck. "What do you mean by famous?" he inquires.

"Oh, don't deny it! We know all the aces of Section 17 by name. We know the Kaiser gave three of you the ' Pour le Mérite ' Order for excellent long-distance reconnaissance work, and you are one of them."

Berger realizes that the Frenchmen are in earnest and blushes. "But really, gentlemen——" he protests.

They refuse to listen. "There is just one thing we would like to know," they tell him. "If you are a knight of this Order, why did you not wear it on your last flight?"

Berger decides not to disillusion them. If they

insist on making him an ace, perhaps it may be easier for him to find an opportunity to escape.

"Oh, that's very simple," he informs them. "It's only a hindrance in a fight to have that thing wobbling about round your neck."

In the course of their friendly conversation his hosts make repeated efforts to glean information of military importance by apparently innocent questions and skilful traps. Berger joyfully utilizes the happy chance to pull their legs.

After lunch they take great pride in showing him their photographs of German aerodromes, fieldworks, etc. "Our prints reveal all the secrets of your leaders," they assure him.

Berger laughs at them. "If you'll allow me to speak frankly, gentlemen—anyone of us who came home with such poor photos would be sacked from the air service for incompetence and sent back to the trenches."

The Frenchmen agree with him humbly. "Yes, if we only had instruments like your Zeiss and Goerz," they sigh.

Later in the afternoon the *aviateurs* bid farewell to their German colleague.

"You have seen, my dear comrade, that we know how to honour a valiant foeman. We sincerely regret that we have no influence on your future prospects. If you should be badly treated, we beg you not to blame it on to us."

Berger says good-bye to all of them with words of genuine gratitude.

. . . . .

The following day he undergoes his third examination. As formerly, he refuses to answer any questions. The general in command of the army corps is there in person; when this worthy becomes insistent, Berger gives him a piece of his mind. Result: in addition to the usual three weeks cells for refusal to answer questions he gets a similar sentence for "lack of proper respect."

. . . . .

The Entente are so pleased at having at last caught the great airman, Berger, that their illustrated papers deal worthily with his capture. The French papers publish his portrait with a huge headline " UN AS DES AVIATEURS BOCHES," while an English magazine prefaces with the title of " AN OVERBOLD GERMAN FLYER " a biography that an imaginative reporter has conjured up with his pen. It is pure fiction from beginning to end.

. . . . .

Epilogue.

Berger returned from captivity in February 1920, and was stationed at Breslau.

On April 20, 1921, he was ordered to act as observer in a machine which was to be piloted to Hamburg when the Inter-Allied Military Commission released it for the use of the Heligoland Observatory.

However this L.V.G. got into a spin shortly after taking off and crashed with the engine on. The machine went to the devil—and Berger nearly went to heaven. (Photograph 17.) His case was a most interesting one from the medical point of view.

HONOURING A HERO

Arms dislocated.
Shoulderblades wrenched apart.
Six leg fractures.
All ribs broken.
Cheekbone fracture.
Upper jaw fracture.
Nose fracture.
Skull fracture.
Spinal column : two fractures.

Nevertheless a complete man was rebuilt from the wreckage with the aid of the " plaster boxes." He could even walk without human assistance and—later on—even without crutches. A psychical element played a great part in this triumph of surgery, for six weeks after his crash Berger—still encased in plaster—announced his engagement to the young lady who nursed him.

Woman's love even overcame the wrath of Destiny, for henceforth Berger had no more bad luck in the air.

The chief reason for this, however, was the fact that before his wedding he had solemnly to promise his little bride that he would never get inside a machine again.

CHAPTER XIV

P.G.

*P*RISONNIER *de guerre!*

Stattaus was consigned to the prison at Châlons where he had to serve his twenty-one days for refusing to answer questions. He shook his head in perplexity. To punish a prisoner of war for behaving like an honourable soldier—that was really a dirty trick!

He inspected his new apartment. It measured only two by four and a half metres.

The barred window was located so high up that he could not look out of it. The furniture consisted of an iron bedstead, a chair and a little table, with a spoon attached to a chain. All these articles were folding ones.

A rasping noise at the door. Someone opens the outer shutter of the peephole and takes stock of the new inmate. Stattaus indignantly turns his back on the peeper in order to give him no scope for his odious inquisitiveness. Then he hears loud steps approaching. A shutter is opened; bread and soup are thrust inside. Only an arm is visible. This is the usual procedure at all mealtimes.

This monotony is terrible after the joyous camaraderie in Attigny and the exciting flights in the enemy's country. The only possible activity open to him is to walk round and round his cell. Round and round by the right for hours; left turn when the ankles begin to ache. That at least engenders a beneficial fatigue which sends him to sleep at night.

Stattaus remembers an experience of his youth. When he saw lions and tigers for the first time in the Königsberg Zoo—saw them pacing up and down restlessly behind the bars, he wondered pityingly: "How can a creature accustomed to freedom stick such a life?" And now he is in the same plight.

The body can be forced into exhaustion by the rounds, but the mind refuses to slumber. Awake or asleep, it pines and frets. Stattaus is carved of hard wood, but often in these days there are tears in his eyes.

At last, on the fifth day, the cell door is thrown open. The warder appears and conducts the prisoner to an officer. The old game of questions begins anew. They hope to have tamed him by solitary confinement. But Stattaus remains unbroken.

"It is useless asking me any more questions. If you were our prisoner and we tried to pump you, you would refuse to give us any information about military affairs."

Again and again the *capitaine* tries to get something out of the obstinate fellow. Finally he makes an effort to get the conversation going by talking as one expert to another.

"I have often flown over enemy territory myself. As I am therefore in a position to judge, I am surprised to find the German airmen crossing our lines so seldom. Probably they are afraid of our immense superiority."

Stattaus feels his airman's honour attacked and promptly thaws.

"What? We never dare to cross the lines? Why, my section alone sends a machine on a long-distance reconnaissance across the Marne at least twice a day. And as for your French superiority—well, you may be superior in numbers, but it's strange that your scouts never dare attack our solitary reconnaissance machines singlehanded—no, not even when we're thirty kilometres behind your lines. They only risk it when there are two or three of them together."

Now it is the French captain's turn to feel injured. "But you're so taken up with looking out for our scouts," he protests, "that you can never make any observations."

This is a welcome cue to Stattaus. He replies, with a hearty laugh:

"I fancy our general staff gets much better information about your plans from us airmen than your staff gets about ours. For instance, we reported your new squadron aerodrome at Matouges weeks ago—and the completion of the Noblette-Auves valley railway as well."

He enjoys the satisfaction of administering an unpleasant surprise to his inquisitor, who breaks off the examination.

. . . . .

Several days later Stattaus is allowed a breath of fresh air for the first time. He is permitted to walk in the prison yard. Even though it measures only four metres by eight, what a joy to see a bit of blue sky again!

While he draws deep breaths and paces up and down with slow steps he hears a door opening. Does that mean he must go back to his cell after only a couple of minutes outside? He turns round dejectedly—and can hardly believe his eyes. A man in field-grey!

Hearty greetings. Stattaus is happy to speak German with a German. An exchange of war experiences follows. The lance-corporal went into action with the 140th and was taken prisoner as far back as 1914.

" And have you been in prison here all that time?"

The lance-corporal protests. "Oh no! They sent me to a labour company straight off. But I got up to mischief there, and they gave me four weeks for it."

After a furtive glance round he draws a packet of cigarettes from his pocket. "Like a smoke?"

He has also a box of matches handy.

Stattaus is in heaven. Something to smoke again

at last! He inhales the long-missed smoke with thorough enjoyment.

When the lance-corporal has given an account of his captivity and expressed his feelings profanely about the horrible conditions in the labour company, Stattaus describes the adventure of his last flight. Their conversation lasts out three cigarettes; then the door opens and the warder appears.

Stattaus sees the packet of cigarettes vanish with genuine regret.

"See you again to-morrow!" the lance-corporal whispers to him as he goes in.

. . . . .

Couched on his iron bedstead that evening, Stattaus meditates on the incidents of that eventful day before falling off to sleep.

He hopes he will meet the man again to-morrow. Certainly he must seriously consider whether as a sergeant he can accept cigarettes from a lance-corporal. But, after all, all rank is dropped in captivity. Those smokes were glorious. How did the lance manage to get hold of them?

Stattaus begins to ponder this problem. What are the French up to—allowing this man to go about with tobacco?

When a most incomprehensible restlessness has driven him to resume his rounds in the dark, a ray of light penetrates to his brain. This is a trick! The 140th foot? Yes, wasn't that regiment in Alsace? Probably the man is a deserter whom the French put with German prisoners so that they can pour out their hearts to him!

17. BERGER'S LAST CRASH.

18. GOY'S MACHINE AFTER BEING PATCHED UP.

Yes, that must be it!

And then he also remembers that he has heard of that sort of thing when he was in Attigny. He considers: has he let anything out to the swine? No, thank Heaven, not yet! The blighter told him a few tales about his own " captivity," and in return he only gave him the story of his last flight. Then the warder came.

Stattaus draws a deep breath of relief.

He hopes he will meet the fellow again to-morrow. Then he can give him a piece of his mind. But first he must diddle a couple more of those cigarettes out of him.

His mind being at ease, Stattaus throws himself on his bed again. He falls asleep with a happy smile of malicious glee.

. . . . .

No sooner planned than done.

When he is escorted to the yard the following morning, it is not long before the lance-corporal comes tripping in. Immediately after their mutual greetings he extracts a new packet of ten from his pocket. A few seconds later the delicate blue smoke curls upward beyond the bare walls.

The lance-corporal picks up the threads of yesterday's conversation most adroitly. But Stattaus manages to divert him again and again with the questions he interposes. Not until they have reached the fourth cigarette does the lance-corporal proceed to an energetic offensive.

" Where's your section stationed? " he asks.

" At Sedan! "

"At Sedan? So far behind the lines?"

Stattaus proceeds to further lies without turning an eyelash. "We have first-class machines that can easily do their 220 kilometres an hour and climb 5,000 in fifteen minutes with two hundredweight of bombs on board. That's something to send the Frenchies running to their holes."

The lance-corporal's mouth opens widely. "Donnerwetter! And how many sections have you got in the Champagne?"

Stattaus considers the question. As a matter of fact there are only seven, but he can afford to draw the long bow a bit. He counts them off on his fingers.

"At least twenty; perhaps twenty-one!"

Greater and greater is the lance-corporal's amazement. "It's impossible. Where are they all stationed?"

"I've seen the aerodromes often enough from the air. But I don't know the names of the places. I can only tell you where our own section is."

"And where's that?"

Meanwhile Stattaus has finished his fourth cigarette and regards its tiny stump thoughtfully. The lance-corporal dutifully offers him another. As Stattaus knows that the supply is now exhausted, he has no further desire for conversation with the loathsome fellow and so puts a speedy end to it.

"Where my section is? In Bazancourt!"

The lance-corporal's face grows red. An awkward pause. At last he pulls himself together.

"That's not right. You said it was in Sedan just now!"

Stattaus gives him a friendly grin. " Yes, of course I said that ! "

" But how am I to understand the contradiction ? "

" That's not very difficult. I lied before."

" But now you are telling the truth ? "

" Am I ? No, I'm telling more lies. Just as you are, for never in my life can I believe you are a German lance-corporal."

When the subsequent discussion grows lively the warder appears with a wooden face and escorts Stattaus back to his cell.

From that day onward he is not allowed in the yard any more. He has no further conversation with the " lance-corporal "—and consequently gets nothing more to smoke.

That is certainly a pity.

. . . . .

Once more boredom invades the little cell.

But a few days later there is a bright break in the monotony. If Stattaus does not see his comrades again, at least he can hear them. Or rather he hears the anti-aircraft batteries of Châlons firing ! And at whom should they be shooting if not some airman of the dear old 17 out on a long distance reconnaissance ? Hurrah !

On every day of flying weather the joyful sounds reach his ears.

Often Stattaus counts the rounds, adding them up sometimes to more than a hundred. That reconciles him with his lot to some extent, for if ever so many thousand rounds are needed to bring down one single German machine, the situation is a tolerable one. It is, however, annoying that just he should have fallen a victim to this jubilee round.

Once only dread fear creeps over him. It is to be hoped no comrade drops his hundredweight bomb down on the prison!

But he quickly puts the possibility away from him. The god of chance would not be quite as stupid as that!

. . . . .

But what on earth is there to do when this pleasant break in the monotony is over?

One day he chances to discover something hard in the edge of his tunic. He fingers its outline inquisitively. It is often quite good to have a hole in one's pocket, through which things can slip down and then give pleasant problems to solve a long time afterwards. But what can it be? A cigarette? No, too hard for that!

Stattaus pushes it carefully up to daylight.

A pencil!

If he only had paper as well, he could write his memoirs. But that would be all in vain, because the French would take the manuscript away. But the whitewashed walls of his cell will serve. So why not draw a fresco? The subject? It must be something that will impress the French. After some reflection a good idea occurs to him.

Lieutenant Barth, with whom he flew formerly, was rightly known as a man of foresight. Not only did he work out accurately with his slide-rule the effect of the wind's drift on his flights and the allowance he must make when dropping his bombs, but he also gave his pilots instructions in the geography of our Champagne sector.

"You must have the whole map in your head," he would tell them, "so that you can bring the machine home again unaided if I am badly wounded or finished off."

Through the regular instruction he received Stattaus knew by heart not only the front positions but also the French hinterland. That was something which would enable him to inspire the French with a proper respect for the airmen of No. 17! So he took his pencil and drew a map of our reconnaissance area on the whitewashed wall.

The next day the warder watched him at work through the peephole, just as he was putting the finishing touches. Full of curiosity, he entered and planted himself with outstretched legs before the sketch. Having studied it thoroughly, he turned round to Stattaus and uttered one single word of admiration:

"Olala!"

In the course of the day his colleagues and even the Intelligence Officer came to marvel at the accuracy of the map. Recognition of merit is a universal virtue; in this case it had the effect of saving the dauber of walls from any punishment and even from an admonishment " for damaging state property."

．　．　．　．　．

When Stattaus has finished his three weeks, he is sent off by train to the distribution camp at Connantray. He is heartily glad that the depressing solitary confinement is over.

The accommodation, however, is worse than in the

prison. The huts are merely knocked together with boards and roofed over with damaged beaver-boards. The windows are not made of glass, but of impregnated linen. As the wind forces them open, the prisoners have to huddle together in the more or less dry central portion of the hut when it rains.

The water-supply is likewise unsatisfactory. The three springs deliver scarcely sufficient quantities for kitchen purposes. Anyone wanting to wash must wait until sufficient liquid has trickled through. If he cannot hold out so long, he may go unwashed for days.

Cold, damp, and lack of hygiene make dysentery a constant occurrence. Apart from these factors a sojourn in this camp is more or less pleasant, as it is supposed to be a recuperation camp. Prisoners are allowed a bath when they enter and even receive clean underwear.

Moreover, the food is quite palatable. Some comrades, however, do not get enough of it to still their hunger, as for instance, Ensign von Schwenen, who has reached the stately height of two metres in the course of his nineteen years. His messmates have to give him shares of their portions. Some other folk explore the middens daily in search of waste scraps from the kitchen, and are blissfully happy when they find a bone with some shreds of meat still clinging to it. Every now and then the French indulge in the inhuman trick of throwing a few biscuits down among the prisoners. They rush at them like hens at feeding time. Hunger hurts terribly!

Tobacco is not supplied. The cigarette ends

thrown away by the guards are therefore so desirable that men often come to blows over them.

Being a pilot, Stattaus finds himself treated with respect, even by the French, who put him in charge of a hut.

Whenever a new batch of prisoners arrives from the battlefields of Verdun or the Somme and the previous inmates have recovered from their war exertions to some extent, new labour companies are formed and sent to work on railways, roads, dug-outs and reserve positions.

The hour of Stattaus's departure also strikes. After a stay of two months he is transferred to the fortress of Dijon, along with twenty-three other sergeants and ensigns.

When he detrains, he is witness of a pleasing incident. On the next set of rails stands a train that is just about to steam off to the front. The French soldiers jump out to gratify their curiosity with an inspection of the German prisoners. But the men of the trenches are more humane than the base swine and civilian hyenas. They call the Germans *camarade* and give them bread and—better still—cigarettes.

On the other hand the troop of prisoners is insulted by women and even children on its way up to Fort Asnières. They spit at them and pelt them with garbage.

It is almost dusk when they arrive at the little fort. They march in with their escort, and the heavy iron door closes with a crash behind them.

CHAPTER XV

THE RED MACHINE

CAPTAIN Mohr entered the room with excited steps one day when we were all gathered together for lunch.

" A very important job from Army H.Q. Ground and balloon observations report long columns of lorries every afternoon between Châlons and Suippes. What's up? Relief of front-line troops? Reinforcements? Munitions? Gas? And why don't those transports go by rail, as they have always done? So we are ordered to find out where these lorry columns come from. Who's on the second patrol?"

"Schattat and I," Lieutenant Goy announced.

Mohr considered the matter. As the main flying activities of the day were concentrated in the afternoon, the man undertaking this reconnaissance would find the air thick.

"My dear Goy, you've not been with the section long enough for me to send you out alone on this job. So Barth and Kroll will take it on, and you can go along too as their guardian angel."

. . . . .

Both our machines are lucky. They cross the front at Tahure without being spotted by the enemy's barrage patrol.

Goy discovers a Spad droning round over Suippes. As the French are loath to attack single-handed, he does not feel impressed.

But when the pursuer catches him up quickly, Goy has another look at him through his glasses and gets a mild attack of goose-flesh down his back—the machine is painted blood-red. He knows now that the man will attack him single-handed, and that the fight will be a life and death affair. The pilot is one of the greatest French aces—he is Navarre!

Resolved: that he must entice his opponent on to himself, so that Heinrich can carry out his mission. Brief instructions to Schattat: make for St. Hilaire junction!

The ruse succeeds; Navarre follows them. The Spad climbs higher and higher above them—now its nose goes down—it dives. Larger and larger it grows in its furious rush through the air.

Goy gets the red machine in his sights when it is about 500 metres away.

"Tacktacktacktacktack!"

And lo and behold! "Shooting is infectious!" Navarre returns the fire despite the wide distance between them.

Goy has a shock when he hears the bullets rattling all around him. The next moment something hits his body a hard blow—a ricochet, probably.

When Schattat sees that they are in the midst of a hailstorm, he tries to go into a right-hand turn to dodge the worst of it. He kicks the rudder-bar hard—but the machine does not obey him; the controls are shot away. He tries to help himself out of the difficulty with his ailerons, and luckily they get him round. Then he heads straight back for the lines; it would be madness to go on without his rudder.

More shocks: the engine shows signs of distress. "Blubbub! Blubb! Blubb!"

Main tank holed! When Schattat switches on to the gravity tank, the revs. pick up again. But the radiator has been hit too; a shower of fine rain spurts out of it.

Meanwhile Goy stands by his machine-gun, ready to pepper the Spad again as soon as it has followed him into his turn. Seconds pass by—but Navarre does not arrive! He has turned away, and is going down in a glide.

Goy smiles. So he has succeeded in diverting him from Heinrich. But why has this great ace let his sorely pressed opponent slip out of his clutch? Has he got a packet too? Then Goy remembers he has often heard it said that Navarre only attacks once on principle. If he does not finish off his enemy in the first dive, he does not try a second time.

Goy is pleased. What a good idea to take a pot at him when still so far away. If he had got Navarre's burst at a hundred metres, it would have been all up with him.

But he receives a bad shock when he begins to examine his wound. There is a round hole in the front of his flying jacket. Instinctively his hand goes round to his back; when he brings it forward again, his glove is full of blood. Shot through the stomach! So he had better make his will.

But he soon pulls himself together. Even stomach wounds have been known to heal perfectly. Better wait and see.

Once again he searches the sky. If they got into another hot scrap, their battered machine would probably break up in the air. Luckily there is no enemy aircraft in the vicinity, although three French machines are going their rounds.

Ten minutes later they are safely past the Archies of the front, and Schattat brings his wounded observer down and makes a good landing on No. 22's aerodrome in Lessincourt.

. . . . .

When we inspected the riddled machine the following day, we could not understand how the observer managed to remain alive or how the pilot escaped without a scratch. (Photograph 18.)

The doctor gave us very little hope of pulling Goy through, as he was shot in the liver. But his tough constitution survived the crisis, and he made a complete recovery.

CHAPTER XVI

MY LITTLE BLUFF

HAVING visited my old brigade in the trenches on the Rheims front, I got Lieutenant Eisenstück, the regimental adjutant of the 104th Landwehr, to make me a present of five hand-grenades. On my return I showed Engmann these grooved iron balls.

"Orders for the immediate present: keep your mouth shut, so that we don't get stopped using them."

Engmann nodded. "I haven't the least idea what you want to do with them, but naturally I'm all on."

"Every French *aviateur* who tries to have a go at us from below will get one of these things on his nose. If he's near enough, some splinters will fly into his machine—the least he'll think is that his own artillery is butting in to the fight. Result : right about turn ! "

Engmann blinked at me joyfully. " It might be rather painful if it got caught in our tail by mistake and blew our machine's behind off."

I disdainfully declined to consider the idea. " With our luck it would be bound to be a dud in that case."

. . . . .

Lieutenant Fischer returned from the office after dinner. " A clear starry sky," he announced. " That means a big reconnaissance to-morrow."

He grew quite cross when Barth contradicted him. " What do you mean, Heinrich ? There's not a cloud in the sky, and the barometer is going up."

Our recognized weather-prophet brought his lips to a point. " That may be ! But Beckmann's on the early patrol to-morrow—and it has always rained on such occasions."

We all laughed heartily, except Beckmann, whose face was gloomy. No one desired good weather so fervently as he did, because he still lacked a few flights to qualify for his observer's badge and did not want to go home on leave without it.

. . . . .

This time, however, our little Beckmann had luck with the weather. He took off in glorious sunshine, and landed again in glorious sunshine—but there was no sunshine in his heart.

"Unfortunately I did not get to Châlons, because two Spads looked after me over Courtisols. It wasn't a particularly exciting business; they kept a good distance away, and so the slackers only managed to put one bullet into me—but it happened to pip the main tank. We just got home on our gravity tank."

Engmann shook his head sadly. "Why weren't we on that patrol?" he asked.

. . . . .

The following morning the machine on the early patrol returned after an hour's flight.

"Closed cloud ceiling the other side of the lines," was the report.

On other occasions we should have been delighted with such "airman's weather," but that day we were thoroughly disgusted.

When I met my good Take in a drizzle in the course of the afternoon, we did not need many words to express our feelings. He gave me a sorrowful glance, which I acknowledged by screwing my mouth up.

. . . . .

Three days rain—three days jollity for the others—three days bad temper for Engmann and myself. But on the evening of the third day I seized upon the weather forecast with tense excitement:

"Freshening easterly breeze. Clouds decreasing."

At last! And we were on the early patrol!

. . . . .

At breakfast Take stared at me expectantly. "Has the Herr Lieutenant——"

I interrupted him with a laugh and produced one of

the iron balls from my attaché case. Take clutched it with loving hands.

"Come with me, little darling!"

When the orderly entered with the coffee pot, two boys swiftly hid their new toy.

A dead secret!

. . . .

We took off at 6.30 a.m.

When we had climbed above the belt of haze I had a good view of the cloud ceiling that was forming. The wisps were thickening into soft veils, but the wind tore them apart again and pounded their fragments into loose balls. These latter could not retain their forms, but coalesced into huge pads. (Photograph 19.) The distance between them kept on decreasing—and then—coming as a surprise to us in spite of the preliminary notice it had given—there was a compact ceiling below.

A last look at the ground tells me that we have already crossed the lines.

In the glorious sunshine a small shadow plane kept pace with us along the upper surface of the clouds. And since the air was saturated with moisture, the sun conjured up an iridescent halo about our double. It was the first and only time I was privileged to see this fairylike "airman's sun." (Photograph 20.)

After ten minutes' flight we found the clouds thinning out, and it was not long before Châlons and the Marne valley lay unveiled below us. With a joyous anticipation of action we looked about us for enemy aircraft, but just on that day when their coming was most desired they did not come!

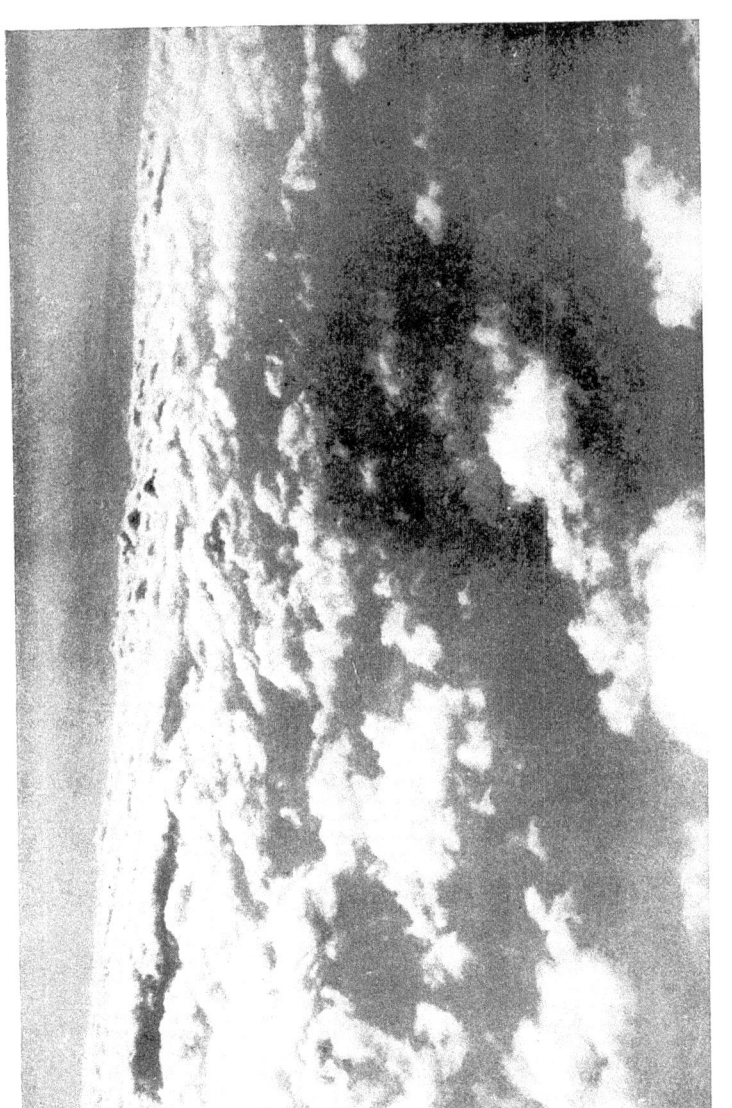

19. A Cloud Ceiling closing up.

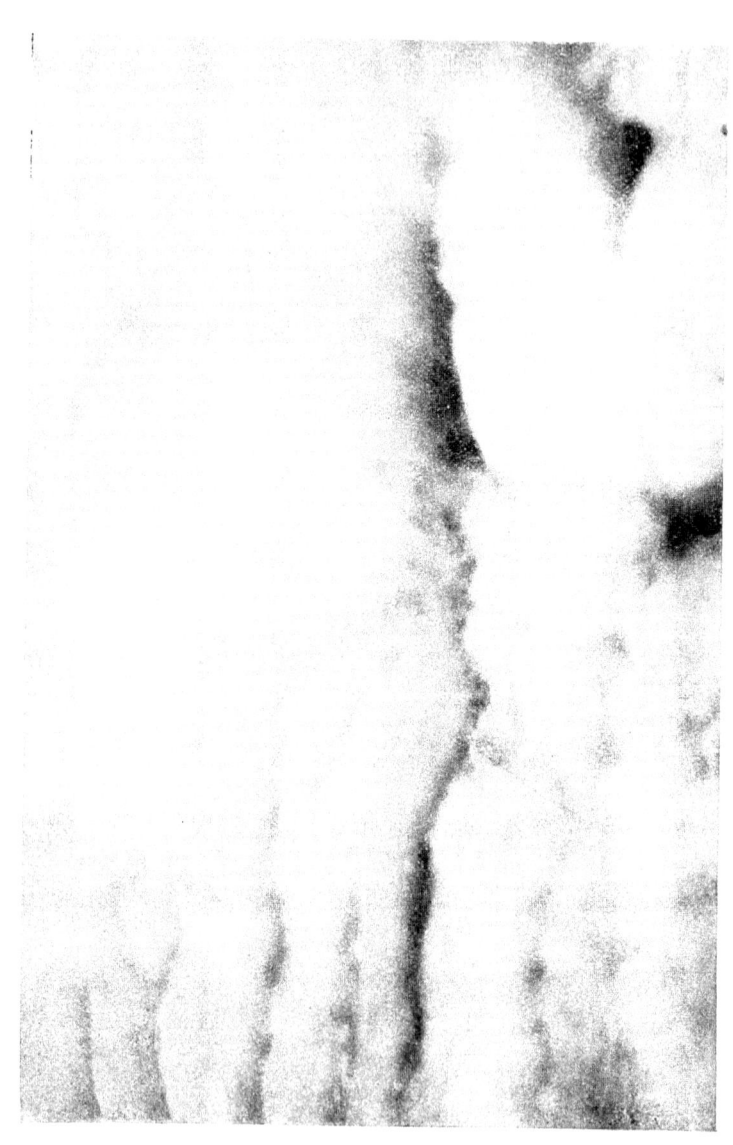

20. The "Airman's Sun" reflected upon an upper cloud ceiling.

MY LITTLE BLUFF

We flew along the Rheims road. Then we took our sorrowful way back to the front once more. When the first shells of the Archies there burst close to us, I grabbed a hand-grenade and hurled it out behind us with all the strength I could muster. Seven seconds later it blossomed up into a lovely explosion.

At last a small compensatory pleasure for us!

. . . . .

All our hopes were centred on the next flight. After dinner Take came into the officers' mess to discuss our orders with me. He laughed when I closed my left eye.

"Dirty work?"

"Photos of Coolus station."

Take nodded approval. Not only were we going to give employment to the anti-aircraft batteries of Châlons, but we would also let the pilots of the Nieuport squadron there have a chance to earn their daily bread.

We did not need to be afraid of having no occasion to test our hand-grenades this trip.

. . . . .

The sun's rays are mirrored on the butt end of my machine-gun when we make for the lines at 2,900. The armoury master has given it such a generous coat of oil that it shines like a slab of fat bacon. Having no desire to get my gloves and jacket smeared all over with the greasy stuff in the course of any fight that may occur, I wipe it off with a handful of tow. But Wilhelm Busch is quite right when he says that:

> "You always find a big surprise
> Waiting where you least surmise."

This surprise is bad enough. My machine-gun is not serviceable! The screws that unite the wooden shoulder-piece to the metal parts have come loose.

What now? Glide down—land—change the gun—and scramble up to 3,000 again? Out of the question! If you want a thing done, you must do it yourself.

I say nothing to my good Take, as I do not want to put the wind up him.

"Fly a wide circle round!" I instruct him.

I hunt for the screwdriver while he puts the machine into a long turn. Always took it along before—and never used it—the very first time I need it—of course I've forgotten it! Out with my pocket knife—jam blade under the edge of a fitting—snap! point breaks off—and I have a ready-made screwdriver. Unload machine-gun—put a screw in—tighten it up—job done!

Unfortunately only half done; when I test the butt end with a mighty shake, the thing comes loose again. The screw-holes are too big to hold the screws.

What next?

I tear a few scraps of paper out of my scribbling-block, chew them up and wedge them in the holes. Then I try the screws again. The next shake gives satisfactory results.

"To the lines!"

We make a wide detour and approach Coolus from the rear. In this way I can take the required photos without getting a single shot from the unpopular Archies there.

They do not cough up their shells and shrapnel until we are well over the town. But the stiff south-wester pushes us out of their range in a few minutes. It is a most welcome breeze in view of the fact that I have not five pfennigs' worth of confidence in my wobbly machine-gun.

Suddenly Engmann gives three chirps with his throttle.

" Trrp ! Trrp ! Trrp ! "

A Frenchman !

Although still climbing, he approaches us at an unpleasant pace.

I feel most uncomfortable at the prospect of a fight to-day. Perhaps we can bluff that Spad, however ? Feeling happy again, I bend over to Engmann.

" We'll attack him ! "

" After drawing him to the front ? "

" No, at once ! "

Take's eyes give me a helpless stare through their goggles. What ? Here—so far behind the lines ? But he divines I have struck some good idea when he sees my grin of delight and laughs as he nods to me. The Frenchman is so surprised when we turn to face him that he remains in Engmann's line of fire for a while.

Then he starts to climb again and opens fire as he dives at our nose.

After flitting past us, close above our heads, he pulls up and turns sharply—a marvellous turn ! This is going to be a ticklish business, and of course I must have an unreliable machine-gun for it !

My bluff has turned out a complete failure. I rattle a few shots at the Frenchman at 500 metres while Engmann dives for the lines. I do not expect to hit him. I only mean to say: "Be careful! I'll pepper you hot if you come any nearer!"

The Spad promptly returns my fire, he approaches, shooting all the time. As I dare not overstrain my wobbly machine-gun, I choke down my nerves and refuse to answer him. At present he can only hit me by a fluke.

The Spad is within 200 metres of us. I shorten my butt end so as to be ready to reply to him—and then he goes into a turn. Probably his gun has jammed.

After flying a complete circle he dives down on us once more. I resume my part in the duet with a heavy heart.

I give him short series of shots. But they do not deter him, and so I change to continuous fire when he comes threateningly near me, shooting all the time.

Suddenly a wave of heat quivers through my body—the butt is loose again. A few more shots—then it breaks away!

When Engmann hears me cease fire, he brings the machine round in a steep left-hand turn to get away from the enemy's burst and then looks round at me. Despite our parlous plight we cannot help laughing at the aspect of my machine-gun. It consists of two parts; one of them hangs in the fork, while the other remains in my hands.

We bolt for the front in a steep dive. The white chalk of the trenches beams at us—then the Spad comes whirling along again. He fastens himself under our tail and spits a burst up at us.

Out with a hand-grenade! I tug at the fuse and hurl the iron ball downwards. A few seconds later a burst develops in the air. It looks most deceptively like an Archie shell—and carries out the deception, for the Frenchman promptly puts his machine into a turn. I sign Engmann to throttle down.

"Bolted! I diddled him!"

Another burst rattles up at us. That young fellow seems to have made up his mind to shoot us down. This time I grab hold of two of the things and smash them at him at three second intervals.

When he sees two "shell-bursts" appearing in the air between us, he finally gives it up as a bad job.

We laugh till the tears come into our eyes. Again I let Engmann throttle down, so as to describe the continuation of the comedy.

"As soon as he lands, our French colleague will naturally ring up his gunners and curse them hard for butting into our fight. Think of his rage when they deny the accusation!"

Joy at the misfortunes of others is the purest form of joy!

CHAPTER XVII

ESCAPE!

STATTAUS was shot down at the end of August. November came, and still he lay immured in Fort Asnières, near Dijon.

Awake or asleep, his thoughts always hovered round one focus-point—escape! A comrade had stolen a small map of southern France from a drunken corporal in Connantray. Stattaus acquired this precious basis for his plans in exchange for cigarette ends and hid it carefully in the front lapel of his tunic.

Unfortunately the prisoners had to undergo a

thorough search immediately after their arrival at Asnières. The map was discovered. Bad luck!

．　．　．　．　．

Even on the railway journey thither they were much puzzled as to the reason why they were pushed off to Dijon instead of being assigned to a labour company. The German prisoners they found in the fort were able to furnish the explanation: Asnières was a so-called "reprisal camp." Whenever it was alleged that French prisoners were badly treated in Germany, their compatriots made life hard for the Germans here.

Worst of all, their scanty rations were cut considerably. When the French guards sat down to a meal in their canteen, the Germans were on the watch outside. As soon as the door opened, dozens of hands were stretched out for the dishes on which there might be some scraps left. In return the Germans had to wash the crockery before returning it. But generally they merely licked it clean.

The black bread was badly baked and so full of moisture that hardly anyone escaped dysentery. The men were not allowed to report sick unless they could show a temperature of at least 100 degrees. Anyone who tried for hospital with less had to pay the penalty with eight days' cells or three hours' punishment drill.

．　．　．　．　．

At the beginning of December another four hundred prisoners taken on the Verdun front arrived from the Souilly penal camp. The worst gifts brought by these new guests were their lice. It became necessary to delouse twice a day. Ensign von Schwenen was the only one who felt it below his dignity to carry out the process. Whenever one of the little beasts ventured into daylight, he merely flicked it off his tunic with a languid gesture.

. . . . .

Later on a working party of eighty men came for a temporary sojourn—men who had been taken prisoners in the first battle of the Marne. They stuck together like pitch and brimstone, so that even the French had a holy respect for them. They had a wonderful way of finding the humorous side of the prisoners' hard life. Here is an example.

The senior of each group always had to report its strength to the French when the roll was called. This was done in the following fashion if no interpreter was there!

"Fifty men present, you silly swine!"

"I'd like to give you a clout on the jaw, fifty men present!"

Their witticisms were inexhaustible. When lined up, the men had almost to bite their tongues off to prevent themselves bursting with delight.

. . . . .

The interpreter was an Alsatian deserter, who harassed the Germans to his heart's content.

One afternoon he summoned the N.C.O.s and officer-aspirants to drill before the French officers. Anyone who did not exert himself sufficiently received blows from his stick. The affair finished up with a parade march,

The camp's senior prisoner, who had looked after his comrades' interests in a marvellous way, was ill and saw the parade from his window. He was white with rage.

"Don't do what the swine tells you," he shouted.

The interpreter promptly reported this remark to the commandant, and the sergeant in question was under arrest a few seconds later. Subsequently he was sentenced to nine months' imprisonment by a court-martial, and served them in a fortress at Grenoble.

The sergeant in charge of the kitchen put extra rations aside for him as long as he was in the cells at Asnières. When the guard had disappeared round a corner, the "prisoner's waiter" for the day thrust the food in through the barred window of the captive comrade's dungeon.

. . . . .

Every now and then the prisoners were allowed into the dry moat for a breath of fresh air. As the stone walls were very high and escape seemed almost impossible, the supervision was not so sharp. Stattaus formed a friendship with the three sergeants Blievernicht (infantry), Hyland (jaeger), and Killgen (artillery).

The main topic of their conversation: escape!

Killgen, who was in charge of the kitchen, undertook the organization.

"We once had an airman here," he told them, "who got away after a fortnight. Unfortunately they nabbed him again because he was too starved to go any further. We must therefore put a bit by from our rations."

. . . . .

They worked away at their preparations methodically.

Despite the gnawing hunger they had to put aside a daily portion of their scanty bread rations. They had only a small compass, which had served as an ornamental attachment to a watch, and a map from an atlas, which was procured by barter. The latter was a poor enough guide, as it showed only the towns, rivers, and railways. Nevertheless, it told them that they had to cross three main lines of railway and two large rivers, the Doubs and the Sâone. They made themselves rücksacks of old bits of cloth, in which each man stored two and a half loaves of bread he had saved and a double portion of meat. In addition they were able to stow away some opium and bandages, together with rugs and ground-sheets. As headcook, Killgen was the possessor of a watch and some matches.

The plan was as follows. The prisoners were housed in an upper storey of the barracks. At the end of the storey below a passage branched off to the tool sheds; this was locked every night. They decided to slink into one of these rooms about four in the afternoon and break out into the courtyard half an hour later, when it would be dusk. About this time the sentries generally went into the guardroom before their reliefs were posted, so that the whole of the fort's interior remained unguarded for a space of some ten minutes.

. . . . .

ESCAPE!

Everything was ready on the first day of the Christmas holidays. Killgen, who was lodged in another room, went across to his three comrades with all his things shortly after the midday meal. As his plan was then realized by his room-mates, three of them wanted to accompany him. He protested vigorously.

"No, boys, it won't do. You've made no preparations; above all, you've saved no grub. And it's much harder for seven to slink through than four!"

But as they refused to be left behind, Killgen was forced to agree.

"Very well, then. We'll help you out, after which you must try to get through on your own!"

All right! The latecomers packed their belongings hastily and went across to the room where the escapers lived.

. . . . .

The main thing was to make a start by getting out of the fort! Despite the strict secrecy they observed the kitchen squad and the other six inmates of Stattaus's room have got wind of the affair. It was certainly not often that any plan was betrayed by carelessness, but in every case of an escape the French pounced upon the men whose beds lay to right and left of the fugitive and gave them fourteen days cells. And that was a bitter business.

Nevertheless their bond of loyalty was so strong that no one was induced to turn traitor by fear of this punishment.

. . . . .

4 p.m.

The first thing is to slink into the tool shed unseen.

That is not so easy because there is always a sentry on duty in the corridor of the upper storey. A student who speaks fluent French is instructed to divert his attention.

The " decoy " strolls out and starts a conversation with the guard. He walks slowly with him to the end of the corridor, when he literally talks the poor fellow into the last room with an unbroken torrent of words and phrases.

They have hardly disappeared inside it before our seven emerge and slink downstairs. They creep cautiously along the lower corridor on tiptoe and pass through the open door into the passage leading to the tool sheds. Their hiding place is secured with a heavy padlock which Hyland has already broken in the course of the morning. Hooked loosely into the lock, the link betrays no sign of damage to a casual observer.

In they go! From within a hand cautiously stretches out to fix the padlock in position again and draw the door to. Then on they go into the depths of the dark adjoining room. It is so full of lumber of all sorts that they have to squeeze themselves together like herrings in a barrel.

Minutes that stretch out into hours. . . .

The sentry will soon make his evening round, to see if all rooms are properly locked. If he is conscientious enough to shake the padlocks and one of them comes apart in his hand, what then? Or if one of them cannot help coughing? Or if anyone should knock against a box in his excitement? Nerve-racking tension!

ESCAPE!

At last—his footsteps!

Slowly they approach. The sentry whistles a tune and slouches along to the end of the passage. Then he returns at a brisk trot. Suddenly he stops. Has he noticed anything suspicious? No, now he resumes his rounds. And at last—at last—heavenly music! he gives the passage door a kick, and it bangs to. The seven stand breathless as they listen in ecstasy to the sound of the key turning in the lock.

. . . . .

The first part of their plan has succeeded; the passage will not be inspected again until early tomorrow morning. Carry on with the programme. They creep back cautiously from the lumber room into the toolshed. The window there is guarded with heavy iron bars and wire netting. Killgen deals with these obstacles quickly. The ladder which they stowed away in the room that morning enables him to work comfortably, while the cobbler's pincers, with which he has thoughtfully provided himself, do good service.

A few minutes later the way out is free. Hyland is the first to force his laborious way through. The others have to assist his body through the small square window with pushes. As it is located five feet above the level of the courtyard outside, he has to drop through head foremost, with outstretched arms. He comes off unhurt, except for a nasty sprain.

Killgen is the last to creep out; before he goes, he passes the ladder through. All seven go down it into the moat. The outer wall on the further side is higher and more difficult to negotiate. As the ladder is not long enough, Stattaus has to gain the crest of the wall with a mighty leap. When he is up, it is easy for him to pull his comrades after him. A minute later the last man is outside—in the open country—free!

A hasty leavetaking. The three latecomers plan to make off to the right, i.e., march due east; the other four mean to bear south for the present and turn off eastwards later. The French will not be looking out for them down there.

"In the homeland, in the homeland, we all shall meet again!"

A final handshake; then the darkness swallows both groups.

CHAPTER XVIII

MERELY BY THE WAY

WE appreciated Captain Mohr, our section commander, most particularly because he invariably got us special recognition for special performances.

His nickname—the townbuilder—had a somewhat bitter taste in my mouth, because he always pushed the supervision of building operations on to me.

Whenever I was not flying or looking after my photographs, I had to be on the aerodrome from early morning until late evening. With the co-operation of our very efficient Sergeant Beil I built the hangars (photograph 21) that were to serve in place of the tents (photograph 22). When all six sheds were occupied, I thought the hour of my release had struck.

"The hangars are finished, captain. Please therefore discharge me from the building department and employ me in the photographic."

The captain screwed up his left eye and regarded me somewhat ungraciously through the eyeglass in his right.

"Who told you we were finished? We are going to make a start with the men's huts now. And there'll be a new job when they are up. You, my dear friend, will naturally remain in charge of the building operations—because you enjoy my complete confidence."

I put my right hand to my cap and replied: "I am deeply honoured by your confidence—but in this particular instance it's a damn nuisance!"

I did not say this, however, until he was well out of earshot.

. . . . .

The townbuilder certainly lived up to his name. When I had built the living huts for our men—and a canteen, with an adjoining messroom as well—I supervised the erection of the technical departments, which included the photography, kitchen, office, armoury, wireless room, lighting plant, etc., etc., etc.

All building possibilities seemed to be definitely exhausted when the last of these wooden apartments was occupied.

They seemed—but the skipper had kept the most pleasant surprise to the last.

"My next task is to pay a tribute to the excellence of your building operations. I cannot express my satisfaction better than by giving you a new order—for a nice little dwelling-house! And what do you think? We'll christen it 'Heydemarck Castle!' And why? Because you are going to live in it."

. . . . .

Ten days later I was in a position to report "Heydemarck Castle" finished. I migrated to the aerodrome with all my belongings that same day. While living in a billet in the little town I had so many jobs pushed on to me with the motto of "You enjoy my complete confidence!" that I thought of myself as a maid of all work, and was snowed under with all the details of my various tasks.

I was builder's foreman—and that is no easy job when a townbuilder is your boss.

I was wireless telegraphy officer—that was not so bad, because our work was long-distance reconnaissance, and we did no spotting for the artillery.

I was bomb officer, and had to be present at every take off to issue the eggs and see them properly stowed aboard.

I had a few other spots of bother to attend to besides these jobs. My pocket book was full of notes, all waiting to be crossed off, but when I migrated to the aerodrome I managed to push them off on to other shoulders gradually and take over the photography department.

. . . . .

Nevertheless the confidence Captain Mohr had placed in me, which had so often proved a sore trial during the building operations, was destined to bear good fruit later on.

We gave him a farewell party that autumn when he was appointed to command Flying Section 30 on Hudova aerodrome, in southern Serbia. We should have all liked to have gone along with him, but that was naturally impossible.

At the party he drew me into a quiet corner about midnight. "I'll get you transferred to me, my dear fellow—because you enjoy my complete confidence."

I made him a bow of gratitude and replied: "In this case I like your confidence"

But naturally I said it under my breath.

. . . . .

Captain Mohr kept his word. I reported to him in Hudova that same winter.

But he showed signs of life to his old section long before my departure—in the shape of a telegram despatched the day after his arrival in southern Serbia:

"How much material necessary for hangar? Send plans and exact estimates by post. Mohr."

You see, a townbuilder cannot slough his skin.

CHAPTER XIX

A GOOD SLICE OF BAD LUCK

WHEN I was working in the photographic department, Lieutenant Barth came in one day in a state of excitement. As Heinrich has no respect for Archies, enemy aircraft, or even his superior officers, I knew something unusual must have happened.

"Are we transferred to Rumania?" I inquired.

Heinrich waved the idea aside disdainfully. "No, but we are going to have a serial camera."

. . . . .

Once again: triumph of the machine over manual labour.

In the early days our cameras only took plates of 9 by 12 centimetres. Later on we worked with 13 by 18 plates. But even with these it was a wearisome business to get a connected serial picture.

A filming apparatus was now built into the observer's seat; it was operated by an aerial turbine. By making fullest use of this it was possible to photograph a stretch of country about four kilometres wide and up to eighty kilometres long on a single trip. That was something worth while!

. . . . .

I give a grunt of satisfaction as we taxi up to the starting point. Glorious sunshine—no haze—that means I shall bring home some good photos. But I say over and over again in my mind the superstitious: "Toi! Toi! Toi!" demanded by the unwritten law which every airman dutifully observes.

When we have taken off I run out a few metres of film by way of trial. Everything seems to be in good order! We cut across the front without receiving a single shot from any of the Archies and are flying at 4,000 metres when we reach the beginning of the strip of territory we have orders to photograph.

I whack Engmann on to our objective and start photographing.

The apparatus hums along at an even pace. So now—all these many kilometres the other side of the lines—I can settle to a real rest. Engmann has directional points that he can easily steer on; the camera will look after the photography business.

21. ATTIGNY AERODROME, WITH THE NEW HANGARS.

22. Side view from the Observer's Seat.

A GOOD SLICE OF BAD LUCK

Archies and enemy aircraft are conspicuous by their absence, so what more could the heart desire?

I take a look round while Take is steering a faultless course. Not a tail to be seen far and wide!

But I get an unpleasant shock when I cast a supervisory eye on the meter of the film apparatus, for the indicator is decidedly below normal. Its movement grows slower and slower—and then it comes to a standstill.

Crouching angrily on the floor of the cockpit, I try to put the damned thing in order again. Evidently the film must have got twisted, because the roller refuses to turn. It means bad luck for the last part of the job! All the same this is a trouble that can only be put right in the dark room.

What horribly bad luck!

I get up sadly and whack Engmann's left shoulder—home again.

But as I bend to do so, my eye glances overboard, and an electric shock sets all my limbs quivering. The turn made by the machine gives me a free field of view in our former direction—and there—barely fifty metres below us—I see four cockades gleaming in the garish sun. As we are compelled to fly a straight course for the photography, the two Spads were able to work their way up to such close proximity under our tails. If that camera had not jammed so hopelessly and if I had sat there for the next few minutes without looking out, we should certainly have been finished off.

The next moment the butt of the machine-gun is at

my cheek, and I am putting a hailstorm of lead into the nearest of the two machines. I can hardly help making a few hits at such close range; the peppered foeman whirls earthward with the motions of a falling leaf.

With the joy of victory I turn my burst on to the other fellow. But his companion's end seems to have made him nervous; in any case he refrains from attacking me and follows the stricken machine in a steep nosedive. I send some bullets after him, but soon cease fire. He has taken such a hasty leave that he is already outside my range.

Then I make Engmann throttle down and tell him the story.

It was a real good piece of bad luck!

CHAPTER XX

THE ACE OF CHÂLONS

IN the course of time we grew quite popular with the good folk of Châlons. Prisoners told us that the reconnoitring machines which appeared over the town twice daily were generally greeted with the words: "Ah, voilà Fritz!"

As we continued to fly over the town despite all

French counter-measures, their airmen gave us the honorary title of "As de Châlons." Even that did not seem to be sufficient, for we received a third name. A Nieuport pilot, whom we had shot down, told us about this second baptism.

"One of us came within a few metres of the 'As de Châlons' in an airfight. When he went into a turn to change a drum, he cast a glance back at the Germans. The observer stood up and he saw that he was an enormously tall man. Since that day we have called the Châlons airman 'Arminius.'"[1] (Photograph 23.)

"Arminius" was certainly Freytag, whose six feet four inches of height was bound to present an impressive appearance.

. . . . .

The telephone started working one day, just as I entered the office to do a bit of work.

"Hallo! Freytag speaking! Morning! Finke and I made an emergency landing at Section 20 in Vrizy. Tough scrap with three Caudrons from Châlons until we reached the lines. Had to cross the trenches low down with the engine shot to pieces and several hits from Archie fire as well; three bits of shrapnel through the propeller alone. Shaved off our battered undercarriage when we landed, and slithered along the grass in the rest of the machine. The good old ship sailed the waves!" (Photograph 24.)

I congratulated him on his lucky escape. "I'll pass the news along to Mohr," I told him. "The

---

[1] Arminius: Latin name for Hermann, the prince of the Cherusci who organized the German revolt against the Roman army of occupation and annihilated Varus and his legions at the Battle of Teutoberg, A.D. 9.—TRANSLATOR'S NOTE,

main thing is how did you two young people come off?"

Freytag laughed. "Not a scratch in the fight nor from the Archies nor through the landing!"

. . . . .

The day after Freytag and Finke returned from leave they were down for the early patrol. The very first flight across the lines and the first flight after returning from leave were always regarded as particularly ticklish; in the first case the airman suffered from inexperience, while in the second he had yet to shake off the joys of home.

In the mess Freytag made inquiries about the comrades who had been wounded before he went on leave. We were able to give him good news.

"All four of them—Pieper, Laucke, Steinbrenner and Berger are mending nicely."

"Topping! Any further casualties?"

This time our news was not so good. "Another four wounded in the last four weeks. Casparito: shrapnel in the knee-joint—light. Heydemarck: scratch on left hand from machine-gun bullet—light. Kretzschmar: machine-gun bullet through right leg—light. And then unfortunately Goy: shot through stomach in airfight with Navarre—severe!"

Freytag pulled a long face. "Dirty work! And who was up to-day?"

I gave a brief report of my flight. "Fight with two Nieuports over Ménehould. But they broke it off because their own Archies kept butting in."

Freytag laughed. "Hope I have the same luck to-morrow!"

. . . . .

But the skipper received me with a gloomy face when I arrived at the aerodrome the following morning.

"A report from the balloons. Freytag and Finke downed in a fight."

Not long afterwards a French airman dropped a letter, which was written in German :

July 28, 1916.

To Flying Section 17.

. . . . .

The French airmen have to inform you that Lieutenant Freytag and Corporal Finke died as heroes in a fight in the air at 5 a.m. on July 27th.

Their remains were buried with military honours at the cemetery in Minaucourt.

Three days later there was a full report in the French wireless news from Lyons :

Some details of the heroic end of our airman, Marquart de Terline.

When a German machine was seen to cross the lines about 4 a.m. on the morning of July 27th and make for Châlons, three French scouts took off to intercept it. As soon as the German caught sight of them, he turned and went back to the front. The three Frenchmen pursued and attacked him with their machine-guns, but two of them were soon forced to land, so that Marquart de Terline's Nieuport was left to face the Albatros which carried a crew of two.

The very evening before, this airman had remarked

THE ACE OF CHALONS

to his comrades: "If ever my machine-gun fails me, I'll ram the German!"

He was in this plight. Twenty metres below him the enemy was diving full speed for the nearby lines—and the French machine-gun had to remain silent because all its ammunition was spent. To prevent the enemy escaping Marquart de Terline coolly and resolutely put his machine in the same direction and whirled down on the Albatros in a fit of heroic madness. He went down in a dive and rammed the opponent.

The impact was terrific. A deafening crash—and then the fall! The two birds' claws gripped one another; they hung together and whirled earthwards, united, to their doom. Then they let go of one another, as though the Frenchman desired to die alone when the battle was over. The two masses of debris were a hundred metres apart when they crashed down on to the silent earth."

CHAPTER XXI

SCHOOL FOR GREENHORNS

THE greenhorns that came to us from the park to replace casualties were allotted on principle to experienced airmen for their first flights across the lines. The new pilot learnt his job with an old observer, and the new observer with an old pilot.

Necessary as this measure might be, if unnecessary casualties were to be avoided, it proved very difficult to carry out in practice. The pilots and observers

23. CORPORAL FINKS AND LIEUTENANT FREYTAG.

24. THE MACHINE THAT LOST ITS UNDERCARRIAGE.

SCHOOL FOR GREENHORNS

who had been welded to a unity by blood and iron stuck together like pitch and brimstone and could only be torn apart after much loud grumbling. The authorities therefore chose a painless way out of the difficulty by sending them on leave at different times, so that there was always a man free to act as instructor.

In the late summer my friend Take steamed away homewards.

My first flights with raw pilots cost me several pounds of nerves, even though I had the luck to be allotted novices who were technically up to the mark as far as their flying was concerned. But once over the enemy's territory they revealed themselves as the rawest of beginners—as indeed they naturally could not help doing. They misunderstood the meaning of the plainest gesture of the hand or the simplest whack—they had no notion how to diddle the Archie gunners and thread their way past them when there was no helping haze or cloudbank—they simply could not learn how to snake out of the fire of Archies that were on the mark, without losing unnecessary height and distance by going into wide turns—they failed to grasp the idea of always " flying in the sun "—they were incompetent to keep a simultaneous watch on several different aerodromes when flying at 4,000, so as to spot at once any machine that might go up after us—they did not catch sight of enemy aircraft approaching from a distance until I pointed them out or the machine-guns began to rattle—and when we were fighting they either flew straight into the enemy's fire or prevented me from getting a shot at him by going into too pronounced turns.

So when I lost my good Take—even though luckily for four weeks only—I began to realize what he meant to me. He could fathom my intentions without my having to waste many words—and acted accordingly.

And yet I ran up against an exception. Out of every hundred raw pilots, perhaps ten are born with technical flying ability, and of these ten only one is a born war-airman. I had the feeling that I was coaching this one-per-center: He was Lieutenant Kroll, a young schoolmaster from Schleswig-Holstein.

He started his career with No. 17 by writing off a machine most neatly when taking off on his first trial flight. After having received a hot ticking off from our C.O., who was naturally not too pleased, he took me aside.

"In any case I'm not stopping long in your section. As soon as I've done the necessary number of flights in a two-seater, I shall put in for the scout school."

I tried to damp his charming optimism with an allusion to the heap of wreckage he had created. But the " civvy pilot "—as we had dubbed him on account of his after-war plans—was not having any.

"That was a pure chance. All the same I know for certain that I'll be with a Jagdstaffel in six months—and a year later I'll have the ' Pour le mérite ! ' "

I wrinkled my brows. "Kroll, man alive, don't talk rot. You know quite well that you mustn't prophesy your future heroic deeds any more than you can afford to have your photo taken before a flight. That's an old airman's rule which bad experiences have proved correct."

But all my dismal forebodings failed to get him out of his fixed idea. " In eighteen months I'll have it," he repeated.

I felt sure this " challenge to fate " was bound to end badly. But my fears were unnecessary; eighteen months later Kroll really had the " Pour le mérite."

In the further course of the war he showed himself to be bullet-proof, and finished up with thirty-six confirmed victories. He did not meet his doom until twelve years later, when he was carried off by some lung trouble.

. . . . .

My first long-distance reconnaissance with Kroll went off splendidly. Although his rev.-counter went dead before we crossed the lines, he gave a perfect exhibition of flying.

As there was a thick haze in the air and we had the sun behind us, not one of the Châlons Archies fired at us. Wanting to put my novice right as to the lie of the land, I shouted in his ear through the roar of the engine:

" Châlons ! "

Kroll nodded jerkily and put the machine into such a breakneck turn that I had to hold on to the centre section to prevent myself being slung overboard. As he went on turning and turning, I signalled him to throttle down.

" Man alive, d'you think you're a merry-go-round ? What's up ? "

He gave me a look which showed he was deeply offended. " Why, you said ' Canons ! ' just now. And only yesterday someone was telling me I had to make the Archie's job harder for them by going into turns!"

As we were thirty kilometres behind the lines, we had to count on the possibility of a fight any moment. But we laughed till our sides ached when the trifling misunderstanding was cleared up.

. . . . .

As Kroll needed no further tuition, he was allotted to Holzhausen, although I would have gladly kept him until my good Take returned.

Then Lance-Corporal Schattat was assigned to me as my pilot, and I got on very well with him too. He was a handy fellow, who likewise "flew a clean propeller."

Unfortunately he was killed in an airfight a few months later.

25. LANCE-COPORAL SCHATTAT (ON THE RIGHT!)

26. CUMULI.

CHAPTER XXII

THE LUCK OF THE CLOUDS

THERE was a short spell of rain in the middle of August.

Clouds, clouds, clouds!

They looked as if you could touch them as they chased each other day after day across the wet slate roofs of Attigny. We beamed.

" Glorious airman's weather ! "

One of our greenhorns did not see the point of this remark.

" What ! You call this piggish weather ' airman's weather ! ' I shouldn't like to be up now ! "

A joyful peal of laughter rewarded his simplicity. Heinrich—the born schoolmaster—explained the difference to him.

"This is what you've got to remember : 'airman's weather' is the sort of weather the airman likes, because he hasn't got to fly. 'Flying weather,' on the other hand, makes him curse, because he has to go up in it."

.   .   .   .   .

The service book went round after dinner.

"Who's on the early patrol?" inquired Lieutenant Holzhausen across the table.

"Heydemarck and Schattat!" (Photograph 25.)

He laughed at me until his great teeth gleamed and his blue eyes almost disappeared.

"Well, that's certain to come off! You two'll have to stick it in silent heroism!"

Heinrich rose and went over to the barometer without a word. He gave its glass three or four tender taps. When the slim hand gave a slight downward quiver, he turned round with a grin that should have made any further questions unnecessary.

"Well, Heinrich?"

He brought his mouth to a point as an additional sign of inward satisfaction and raised his index finger.

"Wooonn—der—fuuull!"

.   .   .   .   .

It was not merely a good thing but rather an absolute necessity when we got some "airman's weather" again after long spells of fine days. The nerves that were bound to be affected in time by

THE LUCK OF THE CLOUDS

constant fighting and heavy losses had to have some chance to recuperate.

Then, when the sun shone again, we were fresh and burning with ambition.

But this time the spell of bad weather was a bit too long. For seven whole days no one could take off.

I called up the meteorological station on the afternoon of the seventh.

"A deep depression from the north. No prospect of improvement."

I passed the news on to Schattat sadly.

"That's a whole week that none of us has been able to show himself on the other side of the lines. The fellow who flies the first patrol will get a good laugh. If he keeps his eyes skinned, he'll see a whole heap of new things!"

. . . . .

It was raining the next morning. But the weather forecast was good.

"The depression is moving. Clouds up to 6,000. Tendency to thunderstorms."

I wander off to the aerodrome with Schattat when the rain began to abate about noon.

"I think there'll be something doing. The clouds have grown much thinner."

Schattat laughs. "Hope is a blessed thing!"

But my optimism is rewarded. The clouds are parting and showing a splash of blue. So into the machine quickly, and off!

We break through the lowest layer of clouds at 1,800. A look round gives me food for thought; to northward of the Aisne I see a steep black wall with jagged edges, from which flash after flash quivers—a heavy thunderstorm! Luckily it does not cover too wide an area; if need be, we can fly round it.

But beyond the lines the cumulus clouds are piled up to such a height that we cannot climb over them. They are over the Rheims forest, where wet sacks of clouds always like to hook on to the trees.

Poor prospects for observations! There are two layers of cloud below us when we have climbed to barely 3,000. We only get a glimpse of the ground when the gaps in them happen to coincide. As these coincidences occur every now and then, my optimism returns.

We have reached the high towers of cloud over Rheims forest. (Photograph 26.)

Schattat reflects a question into the mirror: through or round them? In response to my gesture he then steers a course for the gaps in the mountains of clouds. We try every trick to worm our way through the valleys between those clouds, but find it difficult to hit them off because the wind is continually pushing them about and altering their shapes. Then we suddenly find ourselves swallowed up in the clouds.

A faint glimmer over yonder—make for it!

Luck is with us; fifteen seconds later we find ourselves in the open. Then we run into a rain-gust. At our present flying speed the smallest drops sting like needles. Ow! Schattat ducks behind his narrow strip of windscreen, while I cover my face with gloved hands. It is nothing like so jolly as the artist has painted it on the mess wall. (Photograph 27.)

27. A RAIN GUST; FRESCO ON MESSROOM WALL.

28. THE NEW RAILWAY LINE.

THE LUCK OF THE CLOUDS 149

At last it passes, leaving us flying in glorious sunshine. Ah!

Flying a south-easterly course, we soon leave the cloud-towers behind us. There is a snow-white plain beneath us. But—splendid!—I see a few dark patches farther ahead.

"Holes! Make for them!"

Unfortunately my joy is somewhat previous. The nearer we go to those patches, the lighter seems to be their colouring; the ground in these parts must be swathed in mist. The poor visibility we obtain for narrow strips of land makes even the discovery of our whereabouts a hard riddle to solve.

But ahead, over yonder, I spy a promising dark patch!

We approach it—nearer and nearer. I stand up and peer ahead, past the engine. And there—I can hardly believe my luck—there is a real hole in the clouds! Already I can get a slanting view of the landscape. Ah! The huge Bessoneau hangars of l'Epine aerodrome!

But—what—is—that?

My hands are trembling. It is indescribably beautiful—gleaming heaps of chalk to north of the hangars! I signal Schattat to throttle down and point them out to him.

"Do you know what that means?"

"Earthworks?"

I laugh. "Certainly! But for what purpose? It's a new main line of railway!"

Snap it! (Photograph 28.)

The first strategic railway built in our sector!

Once again I have the most shameless luck, for that hole is not more than a square kilometre at the most—and I have gone and caught it over the most important part of the Champagne! Half a minute later the wind has driven the clouds across my find again.

On we go! But after having given us such a concentrated essence of herself the goddess of luck becomes drowsy and keeps her cloud-curtain drawn. Nevertheless we slide along our strip of territory with silent hopes of further peepholes. Having no means of locating our whereabouts, I can, however, calculate it fairly well by the time we have been flying.

When I reckon us to be over the Argonne, I whack Schattat into a northerly course.

" Prolonged glide down to 2,000 ! "

There I find the clouds to consist of several layers of stratus, through which we can easily worm our way.

At last, at 1,000 I spy the dark of a wood through the thin veil of the lowest cloud-layer—the Argonne! I hope we have crossed the lines. But when I compare the landscape with my map, a shudder of discomfort creeps down my back—we are over Les Islettes! A wonderfully charming landscape—but twelve good kilometres to the front. (Photograph 29.)

Engine full speed ahead!

We are over the low cloud ceiling again before the Archies begin to shoot—and five minutes afterwards we flit contentedly across the lines.

CHAPTER XXIII

MUST BE DONE

THE following days were full of excitement. The job was always the same—the new railway! What purpose was it to serve? Where did it link up? Where would its terminus be?

But we had to put the curb on our curiosity for a while—clouds, clouds, clouds!

And so a whole fortnight passed, and still we could not track it down.

Our section-commander blinked with joy at me one day, when Schattat and I were due to go up. "The chief of the staff rang me up just now. He wants a serial photo of the new railway."

I glanced at the sky. "I hope it's cloudless over there. Anyhow, we'll see what we can do."

Captain Mohr tapped the leg of his boot with his bamboo cane. "No, no, my dear fellow, seeing alone won't help. You simply mustn't let me down. I promised the chief I'd let him have the snaps to-morrow morning."

"At your orders, Herr Captain!"

. . . . .

Although feeling highly honoured at the captain's confident anticipation of my success, I was far from comfortable about the business. So far it had been the rule for the French airmen to whirl about the air in masses after every cloudy spell, and they were usually pretty cock-a-hoop into the bargain. I might therefore expect some tough scraps with well-fed, well-rested *aviateurs*, so that photography was going to be a very difficult matter.

Yes, if only I had my good Take with me! But at that moment he was enjoying himself in Berlin, while I had to fly with little Schattat. Certainly the latter had developed an exceptional vein of luck. He came off without a scratch when Pieper and Goy were severely wounded behind him—but, as aforesaid, he was evidently luckier than his observers.

Yet these reflections were of a purely platonic character. The order had gone forth, and it was up to me to bring back the photos, so as to avoid letting the captain—and incidentally myself—down at Army H.Q.

. . . . .

When crossing the lines we find ourselves nastily bracketed by three Archies. The direction and elevation of the first shrapnels are so good, that their packets whistle past us barely ten metres away. The blessings that follow are likewise good and ample.

We wind our way through the barrage. Then, after a short breathing space, we come in for a warm welcome from the Mourmelon battery, which passes us on to the Archies at St. Hilaire junction.

Casting a suspicious glance down at St. Etienne aerodrome, I see a one-seater just about to take off after us. His companions will be well on the way up. Cheerful prospects!

It is and always will be a queer sort of sensation to fly on and on into the enemy's country with strict orders to do a job and knowing that the pack is at your heels and the farther behind the lines you go, the better chances they have of shooting you down! What is real courage? With a strange pilot at the stick I have not the slightest inclination for mighty deeds; I would far sooner turn back. But that is not so easy to do on a flight across the lines. Thousands of eyes of friends and foes are looking up at you—and you've simply got to bring back vertical photos of that distant objective. So carry on!

Now I am over the point where the new railway branches off. The white chalk cuttings stand out in sharp contrast to the dark of the fields. By my code of whacks I get Schattat to fly along the line, so that I can photograph it.

At intervals I search the horizon. No Nieuport to be seen yet! I am in luck's way. My tenth plate gives me a continuous serial picture of the line, as far as it has been constructed. Now it is up to me to bring those plates home safely.

We make for the lines!

As the last photographs brought us out not far to the north of Châlons, the Archies there plaster us with shells. I am not so interested in them as in any Nieuports that may be pursuing us. I only hope to goodness that no silly bullet hits any of the exposed plates when the fight starts. A melancholy thought!

Aha, there's the first scout! And No. 2 behind him! Let us hope that the Archie fire which points the direction of our flight will not attract any more of his colleagues!

The French machines grow in size with surprising rapidity. The first climbs past us with a whizz; then he goes into a turn and opens fire as he dives. My shots put the wind up him, and he turns off when still 300 metres away. But he carries on when he attacks a second time, and I have to give him a continuous fire.

When I put a good burst into him, he suddenly sends his machine down onto her nose and dives hard for St. Etienne. I have either wounded him or shot his engine to pieces.

As No. 2 keeps shyly out of range at present, I have leisure to watch the fugitive's progress. His dark silhouette stands out in contrast against some scraps of white cloud.

Ah, No. 2 is now bestirring himself! Unfortunately he has no intention of tackling me in the usual way which his comrade tried with such lack of success, but fastens on underneath my tail. The cunning lad keeps his machine so skilfully in this dead angle that I can hardly get it in my sights for a moment. But all the more plainly do I hear his upward-pivoted machine-gun hammering away above the roar of the engine. (Photograph 30.)

The worst of all, however, is the fact that this dull-witted Schattat flies on straight ahead. He does not even go into the slightest turn when the Frenchman opens fire. The Nieuport pilot must certainly be endowed with a still greater portion of stupidity, because he has not yet managed to put a burst into us in spite of the splendid mark we give him. Just an occasional bullet rattles on our woodwork.

But then I hear a metallic scream to my right. A bullet has hit the strut diagonally from below, where it has splintered. The bits have been pelting like hail on to the upper wing. (Photograph 31.)

My wrath is hot against my fool of a pilot. If I am supposed to educate these children even during an airfight, well then, good night! I give him a mighty whack between the shoulders and shout so loudly in his ear that he can catch my words above the roar of the engine.

"Turn when he shoots!"

He nods, and now at last he acts accordingly. If Engmann had been with me, I should have swung round long ago and attacked the Nieuport, but I dare not risk it with Schattat. I am also furious with myself for not having brought my hand grenades with me on this day of all days.

I exchange shots with my objectionable opponent for nearly a quarter of an hour. Every now and then I put a small burst into him. But with the few shots I fire the possibilities of a hit are all too scanty.

At last, when the Archies of the front hurl their first shells up at us, he gives it up and turns southwards.

. . . . .

Captain Mohr was waiting for me (or rather for my serial photographs) on the aerodrome.

" Well ? "

I kept him on tenterhooks for a while.

" A fight at Châ——"

" Doesn't interest me ! The photos ? "

My smile was sufficient news in itself.

" Well, then, my dear chap ! I didn't promise Army H.Q. too much ! "

. . . . .

Pleasures shared are twofold pleasures.

The French, too, got their satisfaction out of the business, because once again they reported me as shot down in their official communiqué :

" In the Champagne a German aeroplane was seen to fall headlong after a fight."

Nice, but exaggerated.

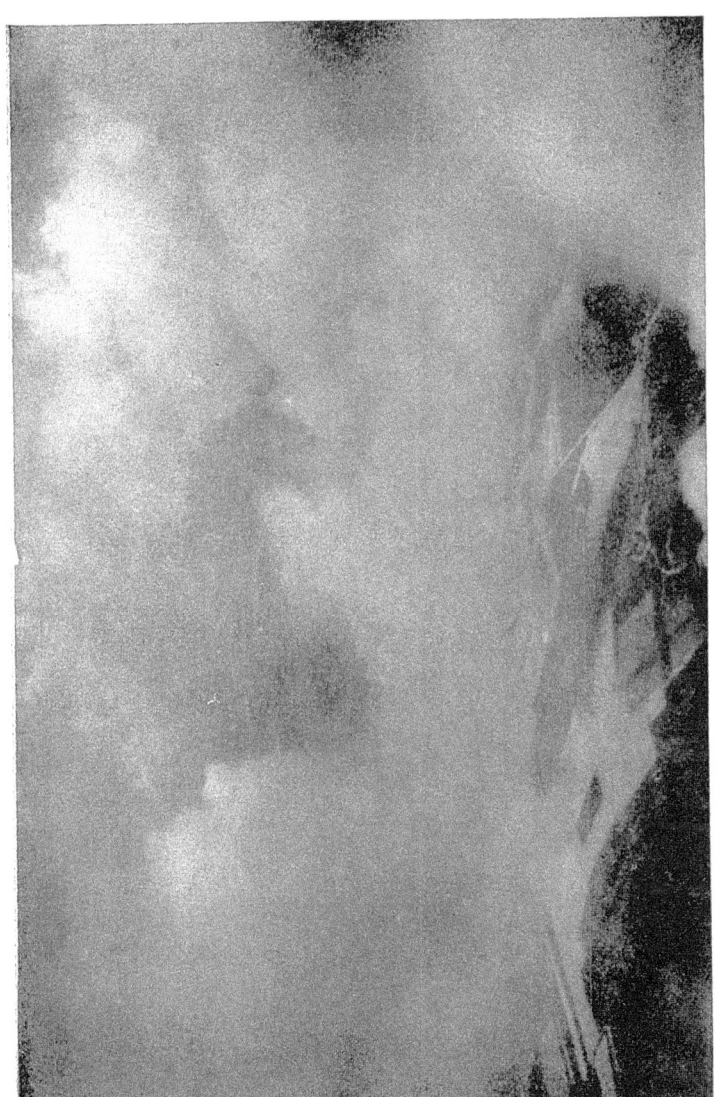

29. RAIN CLOUDS.

30. NIEUPORT, WITH PIVOTABLE MACHINE-GUN.

CHAPTER XXIV

DONE!

TWO days later Lieutenant Sarfert, piloted by Lieutenant Höbel, succeeded in finding the starting point of the new railway that we had been looking for so long—a new junction point at Coolus!

They took off with an almost closed cloud-ceiling and only got snaps of their objective through wisps of clouds. The haze made the landscape almost unrecognizable, but the treacherous heaps of chalk thrown up by the diggers were white enough to take a sharp impression on the sensitive plates. (Photograph 32.)

Their machine was attacked by a squadron of seven one-seaters on the way home. The result was a running fight all the way to the front—a stretch of twenty kilometres. Nevertheless they got home all right, if somewhat the worse for wear.

. . . . .

The next morning our captain conveys this meagre and yet important photograph to the Army H.Q.

The following day the chief of the staff rings him up.

" G.H.Q. wants to know if the two bridges over the Marne and canal at Coolus are finished yet."

Hörnig whirls off an hour later, although the sky is overhung with thick clouds. But he returns in a sad mood.

" Clouds, clouds, clouds ! "

. . . . .

We fare no better the following day. I, however, am by no means displeased with the delay, for meanwhile my good Take has returned from his leave. Despite the rain and gale he and Lieutenant Fischer climb into the new Albatros, which has just arrived from the park.

Its engine is not 160, but 220 h.p.

By the time we are down in orders for the early patrol, Engmann is ready to pilot the new machine over the lines. So on the following morning I stare up at the heavens in anxious excitement.

Clouds, clouds, clouds !

DONE!

"You can't judge by the look of it here. I'll ring up the front and find out what it's like over there!"

And—the news is joyful. "A tendency to clear up!"

. . . . .

Half an hour later we whizz off.

When we have slunk across the lines in a welcome cloudbank I whack Engmann into the direction of Coolus. The farther we fly, the more joyfully beats my heart; the Marne valley before us is quite clear! So I shall be able to bring home some good snaps.

Having searched the air for enemy aircraft, I stamp my feet in my tub and thump my body with my arms. The thermometer has fallen to eleven degrees below. I crouch down in the cockpit, remove crash-helmet and goggles, and rub my frozen face vigorously to bring the blood into circulation again.

The new machine climbs splendidly. After thirty minutes flying we are already up to 3,600.

The Archies do not worry their heads about us at present. Not until we are nearing Châlons do we receive a meagre blessing of some few dozen shells, all of which are wide off the mark.

We reach the Marne at 5,000. Over yonder lies the junction of the lines which Sarfert discovered. And here, straight below my feet, is the place where the railway crosses the river and canal. All of which are clearly visible; the bit of haze can be eliminated from the photograph by the yellow filter—so carry on!

But a mild shock quivers through my bones when I focus the bridges and press the release, for the camera strikes work. I re-wind the focal plane, but it runs down at once. That means I can take no photographs—our flight is useless.

A bitter pill!

So I must content myself with the observations of the naked eye.

"They are building bridges over the Marne and canal. Have traced new line north of Hill 108; it crosses Châlons-Vitry railway at right angles," I can report.

But a great depression takes possession of me after we have landed. I have failed to fulfil the important photographic mission—and not through any obstruction on the part of enemy airmen, but simply because of the treachery of my instrument! Moreover, my nose and left cheek are frozen.

. . . . .

The next day the sky is clouded over once more.

But the following day promises good photographic possibilities. Holzhausen goes up, with Kroll as pilot. He too is lucky, for he reaches Coolus without opposition—he has the further good luck to find the Marne valley free of clouds. But he has bad luck as well—all his photos are useless because light has been filtering into the camera.

. . . . .

Lieutenant Beckmann and Acting-officer Scheidt are the third couple to fly over Coolus. But luck is against Beckmann too, for the third camera fails to do its job. And yet we gave all three cameras a thorough examination, and the trial snaps we took with them were faultless.

. . . . .

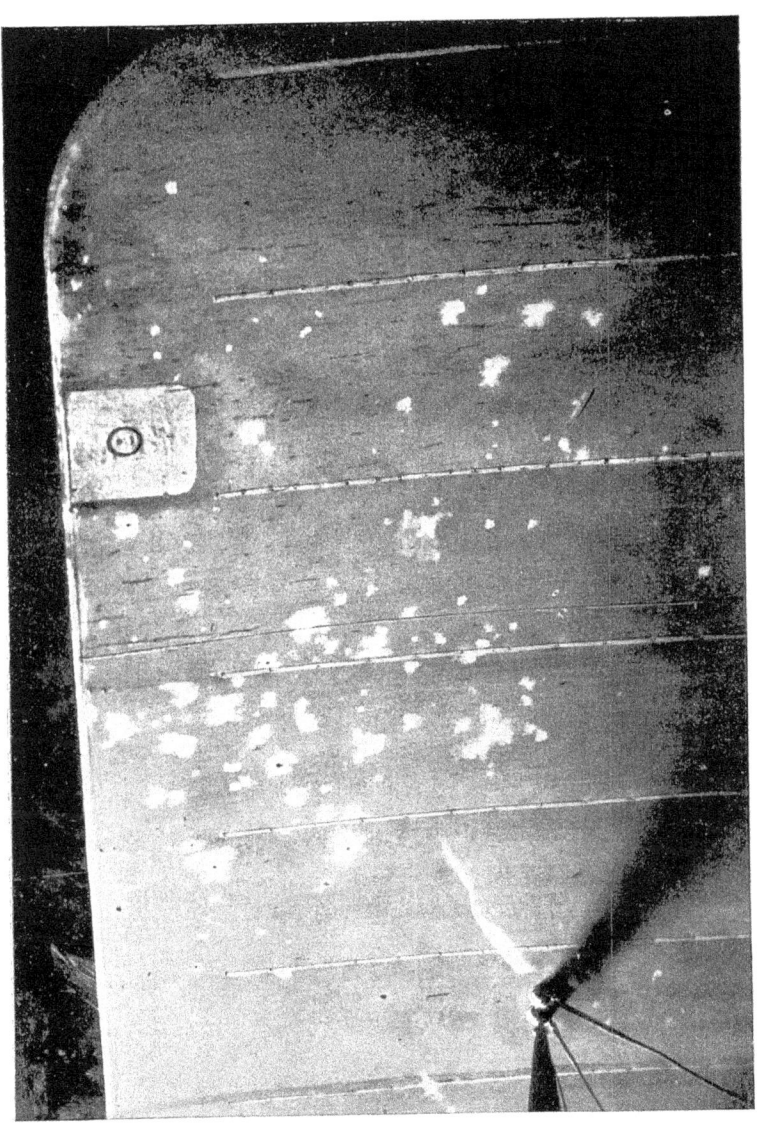

31. WING OF THE AUTHOR'S MACHINE, PITTED WITH BULLET SPLINTERS.

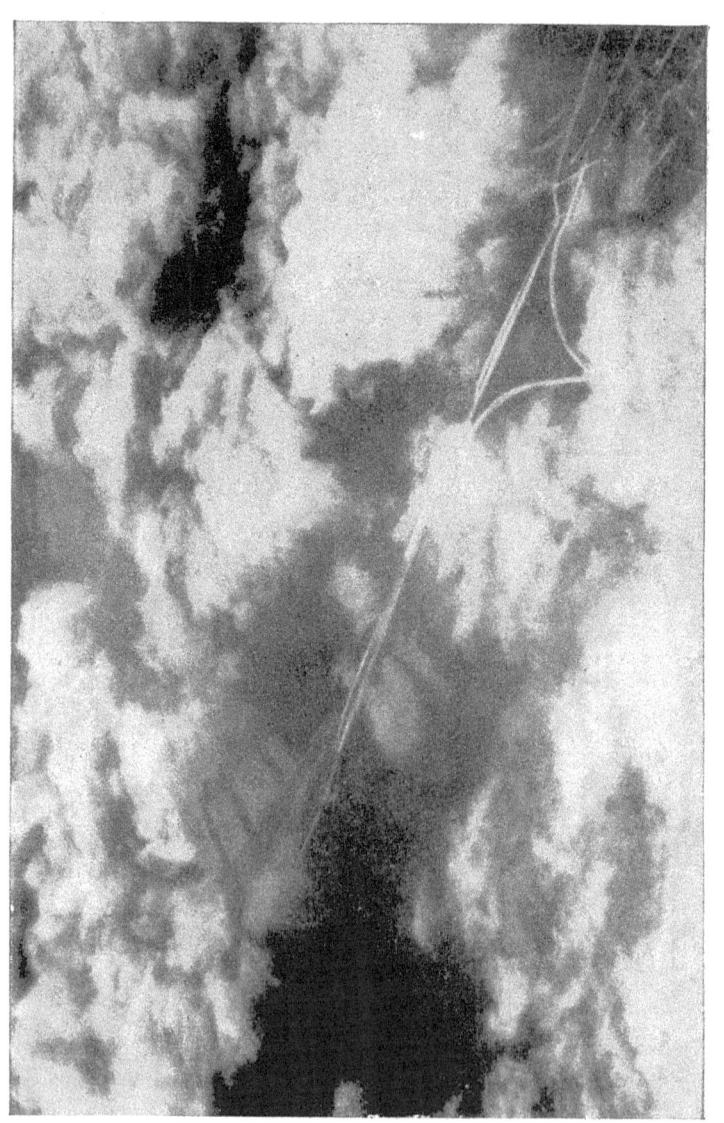

32. New railway junction at Coolus.

DONE!

Engmann and I are on the next patrol. We feel the more certain of success because there is a laughing sun above Attigny. But our faces grow longer and longer as we approach the front. When we have crossed the lines, I find Châlons and the surrounding country are covered by a closed cloud-ceiling.

. . . . .

The weather is clearing up the next day when Holzhausen takes off. It is true that he finds a thick haze on the other side of the lines, with a cloud-bank in process of formation, but he manages the job with the aid of his yellow filter and brings quite useful photos back. They reveal the southern part of the railway, which has not yet been photographed, and all the bridges the enemy is building.

The next morning our section-commander is able to lay before the chief of the staff a complete serial picture of " our " new main line.

All's well that ends well.

CHAPTER XXV

THROUGH THICK AND THIN

STATTAUS broke out of Fort Asnières, near Dijon, at 4.30 p.m. on Christmas Day. He and his comrades Blievernicht, Hyland, and Killgen intended to march southward for the first stages of their flight, turning eastward only on the third night. They were bound for Switzerland.

 . . . . .

The fort is to their left. They cannot see it in the

darkness, but they know that it is there, waiting to swallow them again.

They quicken their steps involuntarily. Their pace grows faster and faster—and suddenly all four break into a run. Their sole desire is to get away, away, away!

They cut across open fields, jumping small obstacles in their way.

A brook. The first man up tries to jump it, but miscalculates the distance in the darkness and splashes into the middle of it. Without pausing to reflect, the others imitate his stupid example. They scramble swiftly up the bank on the further side. They have only one thought—we must gain as long a start as possible! On, on, on!

They go trotting onward. The lights of a village flash up on their right. Round it. They jump a low garden fence. Away, away! . . .

. . . . .

But in the end they cannot keep up the murderous pace that their overstrained nerves dictated. They gradually lose their winds and fall back into a walking step. The ups and downs of the hilly country have pumped all the air out of hearts and lungs. Leaden fatigue creeps into their muscles.

Blievernicht cannot keep on his feet any longer; he drops to the ground. The others gather round him with anxious faces.

"Run along, boys! Leave me here and make sure of getting home yourselves. I can't carry on!"

A consultation.

"Nothing doing! We need a rest too, and we'll stop till you're fit again!"

Out with the rugs. Ah, how good to be able to stretch one's body full length on the ground!

Gradually their strength returns. The church clock of a near-by village starts to strike. "One—two—three—four—five—six—seven—eight—nine!"

They decide to rest for half an hour and then start again. The first night must be fully used to get them as far away from the fort as possible; they cannot continue their march by daylight, as they must keep under cover then. In spite of the cold Stattaus finds his eyes closing.

Then—he suddenly starts up—the others too! Bugle calls—blowing the alarm! the alarm! the alarm!

Now their absence has been noticed at the evening roll-call; now the French are harassing their remaining comrades with questions in their efforts to force them to betray the line of flight. The worst part of it all is the feeling that those bugle-calls are sounding a bare three kilometres away! And yet they have been going for over four hours—at this terrific pace!

Their rest brings them no further ease. Every moment they expect to see their pursuers appear with torches and dogs. They cannot stand it any longer—onward! Blievernicht can already laugh at his fit of weakness—that is a good sign.

"But we must take it easy now, gentlemen! We must keep up an even pace, so that we don't get winded again. It's a hundred kilometres as the crow flies from here to the Swiss frontier; that means a good hundred and fifty on foot. So more haste, less speed!"

Feeling refreshed, they start again. In Indian file. Suddenly Hyland, who is leading, pulls up short. A massive lump of a building looms out of the night. Their limbs quiver feverishly with the shock when they examine it more closely; they are running into the jaws of a fort!

Right about turn! Throwing all good resolutions to the wind, they break into a wild run. Stattaus falls, but picks himself up in an instant. Not until five minutes later do they drop into a walking pace again.

"We must think out our plan of marching. Firstly, we have our little compass to guide us, and then we must make it a principle to keep to the line of the road. We shall naturally proceed at a respectful distance from it."

The lights of a train force their winding way through the landscape.

But where is it bound for? And whence did it come?

The polar star likewise refuses its assistance, because the sky is covered with clouds. Yet these latter offer help of their own, for they reflect the sea of lights of a town—yonder lies Dijon, and over there must be the east. And with that they have found their bearings once more.

But the compass is a bad defaulter. Its hand whirls round madly for a time. When it finally comes to rest, the black varnished tip does not point to the north, but to the west. When they have accustomed themselves to its peculiar behaviour, it changes its opinion unexpectedly and points to the east.

Let it go! The unreliable instrument finds a resting place under a stone. Then they march on at an even pace.

. . . . .

The first rays of light flash up in the villages when dawn breaks at last. Time to look round for a hiding-place. There is a small patch of woodland in the neighbourhood. They unpack their rugs in the thickest part of its undergrowth. But after an hour's rest the bitter cold drives the four of them on to their feet again. They rise, stamp their feet and beat their bodies with their arms.

How to get warm? Necessity is the mother of invention. They pull their empty rücksacks over their frozen feet and lie down as close to one another as possible. That does the trick. From time to time the more favoured inner couple change places with their outer bedfellows.

. . . . .

The short winter's day passes infinitely slowly. All their inmost impulses are urging them onward. On, on! Who can know if the pursuers are not already on their tracks? But prudence bids them hold out in their lair as long as daylight remains.

At last, at last darkness creeps on.

They continue their march at the same even pace; in the grey dawn they seek another hiding place in a protecting wood. The new day is very uncomfortable—it rains! They are happy when they can break camp again in the evening. At least they can feel warm when they are on the march.

· · · · ·

The following day sees them far enough advanced to turn off eastward—in the direction of Switzerland!

This night's march likewise passes off without any untoward incident. They bivouac again at daybreak.

Killgen leaves them for a brief space and returns with a horrified face. What's up? Are the pursuers at their heels? He motions his comrades to the edge of the wood. They slink after him warily and take cover behind the tree trunks.

"Doesn't that village over there with the curious church steeple seem familiar to you?"

The ghastly truth dawns on them—they were here twenty-four hours ago. They have run round in a circle! A whole day wasted!

Hyland cheered their drooping spirits up again. "We must learn from our mistakes. From to-day onwards we must always keep close to roads and railway lines. Then nothing of that sort can happen to us again!"

Whenever a main road crossed the one that gave them their direction, they ascertained their whereabouts from the signposts. As all their matches were used up, the investigator had to climb up the post and spell out with his fingers the letters cast in relief on the cross-pieces. Like a blind man feeling the lettering of Braille type, he was thus able to decipher the names of the places.

· · · · ·

At midnight a signpost told them that the town before them was Auxonne.

"It's a ticklish business now, my lads! The Saône is in front of us, and we have got to get across it. The question is: how? We shall have to go through the middle of the town if we want to cross by the bridge."

To slink through the streets? Too dangerous! How easily they could be stopped by a policeman, a night-watchman or a soldier?

Resolved: to swim the river!

. . . . . .

A long detour round the outside of the suburbs brings them to the river's bank. They gaze at one another dubiously—can it be done here? The downpours of the last few weeks have caused the river to overflow so widely that they cannot see the farther bank.

Stattaus dips his hand in the water; it is icy cold. "Let's see if we can't nab a boat!"

Good idea! They make investigations alongside the bank. But no craft of any sort is to be found.

"We've got to cross it somehow. We don't want to go through Auxonne, and I therefore propose that we march along the bank until we reach the next bridge!"

They have to take the road because the fields and meadows are flooded. But even the road is also flooded in places. They have to wade through water that comes up over their ankles, and can only take their direction from the trees flanking either side of the road.

THROUGH THICK AND THIN

But their perseverance is rewarded—a bridge. Forward and reconnoitre!

No sentinel to be seen.

Over they go!

. . . . .

A patch of woodland takes them to its protecting shelter when day breaks. They pitch their camp in its undergrowth.

But the loud barks of a dog rouse the sleepers a few minutes later. They stare at one another's frozen faces. Those dogs with their sharp noses are more dangerous than men! Voices reach them in their lair, but after a few minutes they die down again. Then they hear a cart rumbling along. A motor-car sounds its horn.

What does it all mean? Why these noises in the middle of the wood?

Stattaus is sent out to reconnoitre.

A minute later he returns, laughing. "We're barely a hundred metres away from the main road!"

They take a line at right angles to the road and march into the depths of the wood. After a quarter of an hour's tramp they reach a sandpit, which offers an ideal sleeping place. Its edges are lined with thick scrub which shuts out the view of its interior. Down they scramble! Out with the rugs and resume the broken slumbers!

But: "All that glitters is not gold!" Not every deserted sandpit is unvisited by mankind.

Their ears are assailed by the whistling of a joyous tune. The startled sleepers rise to their feet. Nearer and nearer comes the tune, and now they see through the bushes a uniformed man, who stares vacantly into the sandpit, in the very direction of their camp.

He is a postman, as they can see by his leather bag. The four lie there like the dead—not a muscle moving. Luckily this trick seems successful, for the postman fails to notice them.

Seconds drag out into minutes. . . .

At last the postman goes on his way, still whistling. When his tune has died away between the trees, the fugitives stuff their belongings into their rücksacks and climb the steep slopes of the pit again. And there they find the solution of the riddle; close to the edge of the pit they find a well-trodden footpath. So away with all speed from here!

They march on through the wood for the next couple of hours. Perhaps the postman really saw them and then feigned ignorance of their presence? Perhaps he has already given the alarm in the next village? Away—away!

. . . . .

The next night they find themselves marching towards a glow of light that reveals the presence of a large town. This time an iron signpost also gives them information:

DOLE

Here, as they know, two stretches of water bar their line of flight—the Doubs river and the Rhine-Rhône canal.

Now the first houses of the town are before them. The illuminated window-panes tell enticing tales of warm rooms and spread tables.

The four take counsel together.

"How are we going to cross the water?"

They will have to go through the town if they mean to use the bridges. Otherwise they must make a detour that may be miles wide. No!

We'll break through!

They slink through the empty streets between 2 and 3 a.m. The time they spend in them seems terribly long. But luck is with them, and no one bars their way. The bridges are crossed—the houses grow sparser—they are in open country once more!

A deep breath of relief!

In the grey dawn Chaux Forest takes them into its shelter.

. . . . .

Here in the woods they can march by day—especially as a kindly mist hangs between the trees. After their nightly stumbles through meadows and ploughed fields it is a pure recreation to tramp the level glades by daylight. But the four are half asleep as they trot along with drooping heads.

Suddenly the sound of hard taps rouses them from their torpor. They look up; barely fifty metres away a verderer is numbering the fallen tree-trunks with his heavy iron stamp—and beside him stands his dog!

The four turn and bolt at once. Luck is kind to them; neither man nor dog notices them. But several minutes elapse before they find confidence to resume their march. They make a wide, respectful detour round the danger point.

. . . . .

Eastward, ever eastward! Once again they have

to get their bearings in order to ascertain the distance they have travelled. They see before them a pearly chain of arc lights—a railway station.

Killgen, who was taken prisoner in 1914 and therefore speaks the best French, must find out the name of this place. He steals up to it in the evening twilight. But no board with the station's name is to be seen anywhere. So he approaches yet nearer.

Emerging from the cover of a shed, he runs into a railway worker, who eyes him distrustfully. Killgen tries to push past him. But the Frenchman smells a rat.

"Espion! espion!" he shouts across to the station buildings, and grasps Killgen firmly by the coat. Officials come running up. Killgen plants his fist in his adversary's face and charges on impetuous feet back to the comrades who lie hid some distance away.

Discovered!

They hurtle into the night at a mad pace. Excited shouts and curses resound behind them. But the sounds soon die away.

The ground they traverse begins to rise. The countryside is so intersected by the works of man that they are forced to take to the road, but not one living soul do they meet in the darkness. Not until the grey dawn of morning—and then they find a woodcutter tramping slowly along ahead of them. Would it be well to rest until the man has disappeared? No! That would be a waste of valuable time. They deem it better to pass him.

Whistling the Marseillaise, they march past him at an even pace. The man calls to them; he wants to join their company. That would never do! Killgen throws a few words of French back at him, and lo—the trick works! The old man does not suspect anything, but merely spits out a few pungent expletives to express his opinion of their rudeness.

At last they reach the top of the rise. Another valley spreads out before them. Down there they must go to-night, and then climb the heights on the other side. A bit of a scramble!

They rest in the wood that day.

. . . . .

After a strenuous night-march down the valley and up the farther hill the morning light shows them a little town at their feet. It is Pontarlier. Once again they must cross a river, and the mountain beyond the town rises to a still greater height. It will be a tough bit of work to scramble up it in the night. And yet—those mountains greet them as heralds of free Switzerland. Their hopes run high—we shall do it—we can't be far away now!

But first there is the river to cross. They can only use the bridge if they decide to pass through the little town. But to swim that raging stream—after all their terrific exertions their enfeebled bodies lack the strength for that. Their provisions were exhausted some days ago; they have made shift to stay their furious hunger with hips and haws and raw winter cabbage. Dysentery gnaws at their entrails. Their opium tablets help them for a while, but at last even this remedy fails to work. All their bandages have been used up.

So there remains only one possibility—to march

through the town! They risk it between 3 and 4 a.m. —and win through.

Keeping to the road, they reach after an hour's tramp a saw-mill that is already (or still?) at work. They creep warily past the brightly illuminated windows that cast broad strips of light on to the road. No one sees them flit past.

For hours they climb and climb.

In the morning twilight they come unexpectedly up against a barbed wire entanglement that stretches across the road. It is flanked by a block-house. Scouts forward! There seem to be no sentries about, and so a wave of the hand motions the others to come on! They creep through a gap in the wire and then resume their march upright.

As day is breaking, they have a good view of their surroundings and can risk tramping along the road. But exhaustion and fatigue are making themselves doubly felt after the stiff climb. Moreover it is bitterly cold up here, where they are more than a thousand metres above sea level.

They spy a quarry not far from the road. It seems to be a disused one, but there is a wooden shanty by it. The door is unlocked; our four are only too delighted to take possession of this castle. But after a brief nap the savage cold drives them to their feet again. They spend the afternoon dosing in the hut; at last the evening twilight steals upon them once more.

On they go. Luckily it is downhill this time! They strike the road again in the valley. Beside it run a railway and a brook, which cross one another again and again.

A brightly-lit town or village looms up before them in the late hours of the evening. They see that they will have to go through it, because it occupies the entire width of the valley. They could hardly have negotiated the steep slopes that flank it by daylight—even if in full enjoyment of their natural strength.

"But our clothes don't look like uniforms now. The people there are much more likely to take us for navvies. So come on!"

There is a letter-box at the first street corner. Hyland calls his comrades to look at it.

"What do you think, my lads? It's painted blue and white—and the French colours are red, white, and blue. And it's got a cross on the coat of arms as well! I believe—yes, I believe we are in Switzerland already. Besides, the barrier at the level crossing was painted blue and white too! Perhaps the frontier was at the barbed wire we got through this morning!"

They march through the streets with increasing joy. The signs over the shops often bear names that sound quite German—such as "Lindemann."

But the next moment their happiness is strewn to the winds. A man wearing a kepi comes round the corner. They turn and hasten away at the double! Having put a hundred metres between him and them, they drop into a walking pace and tramp to the station.

They soon find the board that bears its name:

| FLEURIER |

The four look at one another dubiously. Fleurier sounds most damnably French! But then—what inconceivable happiness!—comes their release from all doubts, for close to the station they see a sign-post, the pointer of which is turned towards the direction whence they have come:

> À LA FRANCE

So back they go—into the little town! Once again they meet the man with the kepi who has put them into such a state of panic just now. Both parties eye one another suspiciously. Killgen advances as their spokesman, while the other three hold aloof—at a respectful distance—yet ready to come to their comrade's rescue if the man in the kepi should dare to arrest him.

"Bon soir, monsieur! Est-ce que nous sommes en Suisse ici?"

But the man feels that they are having a joke with him and goes on his way without deigning to give them an answer.

But when he looks round suspiciously after taking a few steps, Killgen comes up behind him and asks in German:

"Are we on Swiss soil here?"

The official gives his questioner a searching look.

"Yes!" he replies after some hesitation.

Killgen turns round, beaming with joy.

"Switzerland!!!"

The other three hasten up to him and find themselves laughing heartily, for the mighty bunch of keys which the man in the kepi carries tells them that he is neither a soldier nor a gendarme but merely an employé of the Night Watch Association. He becomes quite conversational when he realizes that he is talking to four escaped German prisoners of war. On learning that they have already penetrated twelve kilometres into the French-speaking part of Switzerland, they ask his advice.

" Shall we carry on, or can we report ourselves here ? "

The bearer of the keys allays their fears. " Don't worry, gentlemen ! You'll get a good welcome from us. Go on to Môtiers and report at the police station there."

The four put their best feet forward as it is another three kilometres to their destination. But now that they know themselves to be safe, they begin to realize how tired they are. They take over an hour to cover the short distance on a good road.

Again and again they have to stop and rest.

They do not arrive until after midnight, but receive a kindly welcome from the gendarmes at the station, who give them white bread to eat and boil them a huge jug of chocolate in spite of the lateness of the hour. Then they are supplied with rugs and allowed to rest their limbs on palliasses.

Having slept till noon the next day, they set about making themselves presentable once more. They wash, shave, and have their hair cut.

The news of their arrival has run like wildfire around the little town, and the German-speaking members of the community bring them gifts of sandwiches, chocolate, and cigars.

While on their way to the German consulate in

Bern, they are examined by a Swiss colonel at Neuchâtel. When they have given him the desired information, he inquires their future plans.

"You have a choice of three alternatives, gentlemen," he informs them :
"1. You can report sick.
2. You can ask to be interned in Switzerland.
3. You can go back to Germany.
Which do you want to do ? "
Then all four answered with a joyous laugh :
"Of course, we want to go to Germany ! "

. . . .

So it came to pass—and a few weeks later Stattaus was able to report to me in Macedonia, where I had meanwhile taken command of the German Staffel in Drama.

www.ingramcontent.com/pod-product-compliance
Lightning Source LLC
Chambersburg PA
CBHW070842160426
43192CB00012B/2281